The Elements
of Metaphysics

THE HERITAGE SERIES IN PHILOSOPHY

Tom Regan
North Carolina State University
General Editor

The Elements
of Metaphysics

WILLIAM R. CARTER
North Carolina State University

McGraw-Hill Publishing Company

New York   St. Louis   San Francisco   Auckland   Bogotá
Caracas   Hamburg   Lisbon   London   Madrid   Mexico   Milan
Montreal   New Delhi   Oklahoma City   Paris   San Juan
São Paulo   Singapore   Sydney   Tokyo   Toronto

The Elements of Metaphysics

1 2 3 4 5 6 7 8 9 0 D O C D O C 8 9 4 3 2 1 0 9

ISBN 0-07-557482-9

This book was set in Baskerville by ComCom, Inc.
The editors were Steven Pensinger and Pedro A. Velez.
The cover was designed by Wanda Siedlecka.
R. R. Donnelley & Sons Company was printer and binder.

Excerpt on p. 65 is from *The Life it Brings: One Physicist's Beginnings* by Jeremy
Bernstein. Copyright © 1987 by Jeremy Bernstein. Reprinted by permission of
Ticknor & Fields, a Houghton Mifflin Company. This material appeared in
slightly different form in *The New Yorker,* February 2, 1987.

Cover painting: Alexander Rodchenko, *Non-Objective Painting,* 1919. Oil on
canvas, 33¼ × 28″ Collection, The Museum of Modern Art, New York. Gift of
the artist, through Jay Leyda. Photograph © 1990 The Museum of Modern Art,
New York.

Library of Congress Cataloging-in-Publication Data

Carter, William R.
  The elements of metaphysics/William R. Carter.—1st ed.
    p.   cm.—(The Heritage series in philosophy)
  Bibliography: p.
  Includes index.
  ISBN 0-07-557482-9
  1. Metaphysics.   I. Title   II. Series.
BD111.C34   1989   88-36527
110—dc19

This book is dedicated
to my daughter,
Pam Elizabeth Carter.

Contents

Preface

What follows is a discussion of a number of representative metaphysical questions and some proposed resolutions of these questions. The work is written for beginners, those who have had little or no previous training in philosophy. It goes without saying that one cannot go very deeply into the issues in a work of this sort. I will be satisfied if the book conveys a sense of what the problems are and serves to stimulate logical and clear-headed thought. I hope that it will encourage readers to further pursue the study of metaphysics.

This is not a historical work. I have said very little about the work of such luminous figures as Plato and Aristotle, Descartes, Locke, Berkeley, Hume, and many others. We learn from the past, no less in philosophy than in other fields. Serious readers will recognize this and act accordingly.

I am grateful to many colleagues and friends for support and encouragement, and to the National Endowment for the Humanities for a summer fellowship that supported work on the project. Certainly the book would not have been completed without the patient advice and good comments of Tom Regan.

Finally, I would like to thank the following reviewers for their many helpful comments and suggestions: Gerald J. Galgan, St. Francis College; Florence M. Hetzler, Fordham University; Joshua Hoffman, University of North Carolina—Greensboro; Rhoda H. Kotzin, Michigan State University; and Clyde Lee Miller, SUNY Stony Brook.

William R. Carter

CHAPTER 1

Metaphysics

Metaphysics is the attempt to arrive by rational means at a general picture of the world.

ANTHONY QUINTON, *THE NATURE OF THINGS* (1973)[1]

A person's beliefs form his representation of the world, his desires represent his ends, goals, plans, and intentions. Perception yields new information about the world. . . .

GILBERT HARMON, *THOUGHT* (1973)[2]

1.1   What Is Metaphysics?

The term "metaphysics" can be a bit intimidating. Books concerned with biology or geology start with a clear definition of the subject to be studied. But what is the subject of metaphysics? Different people offer different answers. One view is that *metaphysics is the study of reality.* Though there may be something to this, it is not a beginning that is likely to inspire confidence. The study of reality as opposed to what? Presumably biology and geography are concerned with reality. Are biology and geology then branches of metaphysics? Excluding works of fiction, *every* book purports to be about reality. If metaphysics is the study of reality, then every book and every field of inquiry that focuses upon some dimension of reality is a work of metaphysics. By including too much, this definition conveys too little.

Metaphysics is the study of the way the world is. Though this might sound more promising, it is incredibly inclusive. On the present conception of our subject, biology, geology, and every other field of study you care to mention appears to fall under the heading "metaphysics." To learn that there are spiders in the closet or psychopaths at the bar is to learn something about the way the world is. But in fact such information is not relevant to the subject of metaphysics. Metaphysical judgments say something about the *general* nature or structure of the world we inhabit. The generality requirement disqualifies information concerning spiders in the closet, psychopaths at the bar, or religious fanatics under the bed as metaphysical.

I think this brings us closer to the heart of the matter. But there still are problems. Astronomers, microbiologists, and physicists seek knowledge concerning the general nature and structure of our world. Do discoveries in these fields of inquiry then qualify as *metaphysical* discoveries? Perhaps in a broad sense of the term "metaphysics," the question can be answered affirmatively. However, I will here employ this term in a more restricted sense. On the narrow conception of the subject, *metaphysics is a field of inquiry that focuses attention upon philosophical issues concerning the general nature and structure of the world we inhabit.* Since these questions are not generally addressed by biologists and physicists, such theorists are not engaged in metaphysical inquiry in my restricted sense. Theorists who work with powerful telescopes and microscopes advance immeasurably our understanding of the world in which we live. But it happens that there are important questions that not only are not resolved but are not addressed by research conducted in laboratories and observatories.

On the narrow conception, metaphysics is a subject that is concerned with *philosophical* questions bearing upon the nature and structure of the world we inhabit. Precisely what sort of question qualifies as "philosophical"?

This question is no less difficult than the question "What is metaphysics?" I confess to not having an answer that is both short and illuminating. In the end, perhaps the best way to learn what the subject of microbiology is is to *do* microbiology. My guess is that things work the same way when it comes to understanding what *philosophy* is. We are not likely to learn much from any short definition here. We do better to turn attention to some questions that clearly are *philosophical* questions. If we think soberly and systematically about these questions, then we are "doing" philosophy.

Metaphysics overlaps extensively with nearly every branch of philosophical inquiry. When we pursue problems in the philosophy of psychology, the philosophy of mathematics, the philosophy of religion, or the philosophy of language, we inevitably and quickly encounter metaphysical problems.

Consider the mathematics case. Many mathematical statements are true. Does mathematical truth differ in some important way from truth in, say, geology or biology or international relations? It is true that there are KGB spies living in Washington. It is not too hard to explain what makes this statement true. But what "makes it true" that 5 is a prime number or that $2 + 2 = 4$? What are we talking about when we make such mathematical statements? The natural answer is that we are talking about *numbers*. Fair enough. But what *is* a number? *Are* there really such things as numbers? If not, how can countlessly many statements and beliefs be about numbers? How can important books be written and important discoveries made about numbers if *there are no such things as numbers*?

These are good examples of *philosophical* questions. Such questions obviously concern the philosophy of mathematics. But at the same time, they qualify as clear and indisputable examples of *metaphysical* questions. We may agree that "$2 + 2 = 4$" is a statement that is about numbers and still disagree over the important metaphysical questions here. Some people will deny that there are such things as numbers. Such people should be prepared to explain what they are talking about when they make mathematical assertions. If we are not talking about a number when we say that 5 is prime, what *are* we talking about? One reply is "Nothing." But there are potential problems with this. How can a *true* statement be a statement about *nothing*? And how can "nothing" be a prime number? It seems that anything that is a prime number is *something* (namely, a prime number) and not *nothing*.

1.2   Ontology and Analysis

Similar metaphysical questions arise when we turn attention from mathematical statements to statements concerning religious beliefs. In both cases we quickly encounter questions concerning *ontology* and questions concerning *analysis*. We are addressing ontological issues when we ask whether something is *real* or whether something *exists*.

A. Some questions of ontology:
   (1) Are there such things as numbers?
   (2) Is there such a thing as the number 5?
   (3) Are there supernatural beings?
   (4) Is there such a thing as God?

saying=existence.

When we pose such questions, our concern lies with the *existence* or *nonexistence* of certain kinds of things. To say that there *are* KGB spies is to say that KGB spies exist. To say that there are no prime numbers is to say that prime numbers do not exist. Some people believe that numbers exist only in the mind. Conceivably someone might take a similar view when it comes to supernatural beings, saying that supernatural beings exist only in the mind. If we accept either or both of these claims, we should be prepared to explain what is meant by saying that something "exists only in the mind." As we shall see in Chapter 5, some theorists go so far as to argue that there is a sense in which commonplace things such as tables and oak trees exist only in the mind. Most of us reject this. But if we deny that trees exist only in the mind we should be prepared to explain precisely what we mean when we affirm or deny that something exists only in the mind. Is there really good reason to judge that numbers do and oak trees do not exist only in the mind? Is there good reason to judge that numbers do and God does not exist only in the mind?

Ontological questions are closely tied to questions of analysis, questions of the form "What sort of thing is a —————?" Unless we understand what sort of thing a KGB spy is, we are hardly in a position to judge that there either are or are not any KGB spies. Things work the same way when we turn to numbers and supernatural beings. We can hardly expect to make progress with the ontological questions on list A unless we have answers to the questions of analysis on list B.

B. Some questions of analysis:
    (5) What are numbers?
    (6) What is the number 5?
    (7) What are supernatural beings?
    (8) What (sort of thing) is God?

thing?

Of course there will be disputes as to priorities. Someone might argue that the best way to answer the question "What is a tumor?" is by locating and then examining a tumor. If this is right, it seems that a question of analysis ("What sort of thing is a tumor?") is resolvable only after the ontological question ("Are there tumors?") is settled. Conceivably, a similar position might be adopted when we turn from tumors to supernatural beings.

Thus it might be argued that we cannot hope to answer question (7) until we first encounter a supernatural being. Since we cannot encounter things that do not exist, it appears on this view that questions of ontology must be resolved before questions of analysis can be addressed.

1.3 A Matter of Priorities

However, it is to be doubted that ontological questions enjoy this priority. How can we go about the task of looking for a tumor unless we first know what a tumor is? If we do not know what it is we are looking for, it is very hard to see how we can ever be justified in saying, "Aha, here is a tumor" and commencing with the examination process. The point carries over from tumors to numbers and supernatural beings. In each case, it appears that questions of analysis have a certain priority over questions of ontology.

Although I think this position is correct, it is not without difficulties. Broadly speaking, ontology concerns the question "What is there?" Someone might argue that the very act of giving an analysis of what something is *presupposes* that there is such a thing. Consider the God case. What analysis can be given of what God is? In reply to question (8), some people say that God is the creator of the universe. Once this is said, it may seem silly to even *raise* question (4), the question of God's existence. If God really *is* the creator of the universe, then of course God exists. How could something create the universe and not exist? If God does not exist, God did not create anything. On the other hand, if God *did* create the universe, God must exist. The ontological question may seem to be settled by our analysis of what God is.

Something goes wrong here. Suppose that a child asks what a *unicorn* is. On one analysis, a unicorn is a horselike creature with a horn protruding from its head. Can we then legitimately conclude that there *are* (exist) unicorns? Surely anything that has a horn protruding from its head exists. How could something have a horn protruding from its head and yet not exist? (Compare "How could something be the creator of the universe and not exist?")

This makes it easy—altogether too easy—to establish that various things exist. In fact, unicorns do not exist. When I say this—say that unicorns do not exist—I am saying that the world does not contain unicorns. Our world is inhabited by *pictures* of unicorns and *stories* about unicorns and *thoughts* (images) of unicorns. But in reality unicorns do not exist. There simply are no genuine unicorns.

Thus it is a mistake to judge that the task of analyzing what unicorns are presupposes the reality of unicorns. The important thing to keep in mind here is that analysis generally focuses attention upon *concepts* and not upon individual things. It is a fact that there are no unicorns—no equine individuals having (natural) horns protruding from their heads. Nonetheless there *is*—there really is—a *concept* that is expressed by the word "unicorn." This concept exists, as an abstract object, even though no unicorn exists. Perhaps this concept somehow "exists in the mind."[3] Whether or not that is so, it is the *concept* that we are concerned with when we raise the question of analysis—the question "What sort of thing is a unicorn?" Analysis does not presuppose that there are (exist) any unicorns. What is presupposed is that there is a legitimate *concept* expressed by the word "unicorn."

Of course when we are dealing with commonplace things such as oak trees and psychopaths, it can happen that the task of analysis focuses not upon concepts but upon certain individuals. Having determined that there *are* psychopaths—having answered the ontological question—we can surely hope to learn a good deal about what a psychopath *is* by examining certain individuals and not merely the concept "psychopath." We proceed to learn more and more about "What it is to be a psychopath" by examining certain individuals and not by further analysis of concepts. A concept may be enriched on the basis of examining individual cases to which this concept applies.

But it is doubtful that we can proceed this way when we consider concepts that do not apply to things we can directly observe. Concepts of numbers and of supernatural beings do not seem to apply to things at our very fingertips—things we can study directly. In contrast to the psychopath case, the analysis of concepts and reflection upon the implications of such conceptual analysis seem to be all we have to go on here.

Most ontological questions might be viewed as questions concerning concepts. To see this, we must recognize that some concepts are *instantiated* while others are not. Concept C is instantiated if and only if at least one and perhaps more than one individual falls under C. (C is uninstantiated if and only if C fails to be instantiated.) Since in reality no existing individual falls under the concept expressed by "unicorn," this concept is uninstantiated. Things work differently when we turn from "unicorn" to "lawyer." Since many individuals fall under the latter concept, "lawyer" expresses a multiply instantiated concept. When we say that lawyers *exist*, perhaps this is a way of saying that the concept "lawyer" is instantiated. On this approach, the ontological question "Does God exist?" is really a way of asking whether the concept "God" is instantiated. Here the task of conceptual analysis clearly has priority over the ontological question. We can hardly hope to decide whether concept C is or is not instantiated until we have a precise analysis of C. To have an analysis of the concept expressed by "lawyer" we must know *what it is to be a lawyer*. The same applies to "prime number" and "God." Questions of conceptual analysis presuppose the existence of concepts—presuppose that certain words have an established *sense* or *meaning*—but do not presuppose the existence of things falling under the concepts being analyzed.[4] When we ask whether God exists, we are presupposing the existence of a certain concept—one that is expressed by the word "God"—but we are not presupposing that any individual falls under this concept. Just as "mermaid" may express a legitimate concept even though there are no mermaids, "God" may express a legitimate concept even though God may not exist.

Tough questions arise concerning the nature of concepts themselves. Some traditional theorists maintain that when we speak of the concept expressed by a word, we are speaking of the *meaning* of this word. If this is right, the questions of analysis that appear on list B are questions concerning the meaning of certain words or expressions. It is widely conceded that words such as "unicorn" and "mermaid" have meaning even though they fail to refer to any existing individual. The term "mermaid" expresses a legitimate concept, even though there are in fact no individuals who qualify as legitimate mermaids. More will be said concerning concepts in Chapters 10 and 11.

1.4   Representations of the World

Different people represent or think about the world in different ways. This plain fact raises interesting and important questions. Upon what basis, exactly, can we judge that one way of thinking and speaking about the world is "better" or "worse" than another?

There is a good deal of controversy about this. But it is generally agreed that questions of *accuracy* and *scope* are central to evaluations of a person's representation of the world.

It might be thought that one way of viewing the world is *better* than another when the former is more *accurate* than the latter. This raises a new question. When is one way of viewing the world more accurate than another? A newspaper story is accurate to the extent that the story "tells it like it is." Telling it like it is is a matter of reporting the *facts* concerning a certain specific situation or topic. Perhaps things work the same way when we do metaphysics. It is likely that no two people have precisely the same view of the world, the same way of representing the world. A person's representation of the world consists of a system of beliefs—all the beliefs this person has concerning the world and its inhabitants. Your representation of the world is *accurate* to the extent that it contains *true* beliefs, beliefs that state or correspond to facts; it is *inaccurate* to the extent that it contains false beliefs (beliefs that fail to be factual). Perhaps unavoidably, there will be disagreement as to what the facts are. When it comes to accuracy, each of us is inclined to favor his or her own representation of the world.

This brings us to the question of scope. Your representation of the world is *incomplete* to the extent that it fails to include any beliefs pertaining to some question or issue. Most of us have few, if any, beliefs concerning the gastronomic habits of soldiers in the Napoleonic wars or the true nature of subatomic particles. To the extent that we simply have no beliefs pertaining to a well-formed question, our representation of the world fails to be complete. Incompleteness is no crime. As we shall see in a moment, in one respect it can be a virtue.

No ordinary observer of the cosmic scene has a system of beliefs that offers anything close to a complete—much less completely accurate—representation of the way the world is. Some people are convinced that God's representation of the world has this exalted status. Whether or not that is so, much traditional work in metaphysics has been based upon the conviction that it possible for human observers of the cosmic scene to give a coherent, unified account of the *general* nature of the world. It is important here not to confuse questions of *completeness* and questions of *generality*. Conceivably it might be that Jack's representation of the world is much more complete than Jill's and that Jill's representation is much more general than Jack's. Jill may have many beliefs that bear upon the general nature and structure of the world, whereas Jack has very few or even no such beliefs. It is one thing to believe that the Yankees will win the championship and quite another to believe that supernatural beings do or do not exist. If Jack has a great many beliefs of the former but few beliefs of the latter sort, Jack's system of beliefs may be much more complete than Jill's even though Jill's system is much richer from a metaphysical perspective. The belief that the Yankees will (or will not) win the championship is of no metaphysical relevance. A system of beliefs that is relatively complete concerning baseball statistics may yet be metaphysically impoverished. Similarly, a relatively complete metaphysical representation of the world may have little or nothing to say about third basemen and relief pitchers.

A person's *metaphysical system* consists of a subset of her total system of beliefs—namely, those beliefs that concern the general nature of the world we inhabit. Your metaphysical system (your metaphysical position) is part, though perhaps only a small part, of your representation of the world. In theory, we might hope to arrive at a metaphysics that gives accurate answers to every question, or at least every philosophical question, bearing upon the general nature of the world we inhabit. But can this hope be realized? Is there really a *uniquely* correct metaphysical system of beliefs? This is a higher-order metaphysical question (a meta-metaphysical question) of some importance. I will assume at the outset of our discussion that the question of uniqueness deserves an affirmative answer. (Something will be said about the case for the negative reply in the final chapter.)

1.5 Consistency and Justification

The subject of truth offers rich material for metaphysical inquiry. (More is said concerning truth in Chapter 12.) We might judge that a statement is *true* if and only if it "tells it like it is," *consistent* if and only if it is in theory *possible* that it is true, *justified* if and only if there is good reason to accept it (and no reason to reject it). Such a theory might be extended to beliefs: my belief that S is true if and only if statement S is true, consistent if and only if statement S is consistent, justified if and only if I have good reason to accept statement S. Elementary logic tells us that every meaningful statement is either true or false and that no meaningful statement is both true and false. If this is right, it might appear that the uniqueness question posed in the last paragraph must have an affirmative answer. It is either true or false that God exists (not both). If Jack views the matter one way and Jill another, it seems that one party must be mistaken. There are countless ways of representing the world but (it appears) only one correct way of doing so.

But the plain truth of the matter is that truth is elusive. Just as there may be false beliefs that we are justified in holding, there may be beliefs that are true but for which we have little or no justification. Perhaps (though some people deny this) belief in an afterlife and belief in God's existence are like this. It is one thing to demonstrate that Jack's belief in God (that God exists) is not justified and quite a different thing to demonstrate that his belief is not true. We cannot conclude from the fact that a metaphysical belief is not justified that this belief is not true. It can be true that the butler committed the murder even though the detectives are not justified in believing that he did so. Similarly, it can be true that God exists even though none of us may be justified in believing this.

A metaphysical system is perfectly true if and only if every belief it contains is true. Such a system is true to the extent that it contains true beliefs, false to the extent that it contains false beliefs. To the extent that one has no beliefs concerning a question pertaining to the general nature of the world we inhabit, one's metaphysical system is *incomplete.* Jack's metaphysical outlook is incomplete with respect to the question of God's existence if Jack neither believes nor disbelieves that God exists. If Jack believes that God exists when in fact God does not exist or believes that God does not exist when in fact God does exist, then Jack's metaphysical system contains at least one false belief and so fails to be perfectly true.

We encounter difficult questions when we try to specify what a metaphysical system must be like to be justified. Since such a "system" is made up of various beliefs, we might judge that a metaphysical system is justified if and only if it is made up of *beliefs* that are justified. Some people are offended by talk of justification when it comes to beliefs. Do we not have a right to believe anything we choose? If we have a right to worship as we please (or not worship at all) and if worshiping (or not worshiping) involves believing (or not believing) certain things, it may appear we have a right to believe what we choose. So how can we not be justified in believing what we believe, regardless of what that may be?

This misses the point. The point is, briefly, that when philosophers say that a belief is *justified*, they are claiming that there are good reasons to *accept* what is believed. If we have no good reason to believe that God exists, say, then Gretchen's belief that God exists is not justified (in the relevant sense). Perhaps Gretchen has a right to worship as she pleases and to believe things without reasons or justification. But when we do philosophy, it is reasons that matter.

To be sure, it is likely that there will be sharp disagreement in many cases as to whether there *are* good reasons supporting a certain belief. Any philosopher worthy of her spurs accepts this and is prepared to enter intellectual battle in such cases. But some cases are easy. Suppose that Gretchen exercises her right to believe what she pleases and forms the conviction that a certain Siamese cat created the universe. We may suspect that Gretchen cannot provide any faintly plausible reasons supporting such a belief. If she cannot do this, Gretchen has a belief that is not justified.

A metaphysical system is consistent if and only if not only each belief in this system, considered individually, is possibly true but also it is possible that all the beliefs in this system are jointly true. Obviously a system of beliefs that is consistent may nonetheless not have much of a claim to being justified. Imagine a (very strange) person who believes only that:

(1) Bobby Fischer held the record for most home runs.
(2) Babe Ruth was the world chess champion.

Although this is a radically incomplete representation of the world, it is at least a *consistent* one. However, we can hardly conclude from *this* that we are justified in believing (1) and (2). Obviously consistency does not guarantee that our representation of the world is justified. If my metaphysical system is made up of beliefs for which I have absolutely no justification, then my metaphysical position fails to be justified even if it is consistent. And the fact that I find it comforting to believe something offers no reason at all to suppose that what is believed is true.

Consistency is necessary but not sufficient for justification. Somewhat surprisingly, consistency is hard to come by. Suppose that Jill firmly believes that everything there is—everything that is real—is material. Suppose also that Jill has a friend, Macbeth, who takes hallucinogenic drugs. Jill believes Macbeth when Macbeth reports that he sees a dagger; hence Jill believes that Macbeth sees something. Jill further believes that the object Macbeth sees has no spatial location and that all material objects have a spatial location.[5] In such a case, Jill's system of beliefs seems to be *inconsistent*: if Jill is right in believing (1) that Macbeth sees something that has no spatial location and (2) that every material object has a spatial location, it seems she must be mistaken in believing that everything there is is material.

A metaphysical system is justified to the extent—perhaps *only* to the extent—that its constituent beliefs are either "self-evident," verified by observation, or justified by reason.[6] No doubt some people will claim that God's existence is self-evident and will therefore conclude that we are justified in believing that God exists. I think there is good reason to reject this assessment of the matter. Self-evident beliefs are shared by most rational people. Since many (not all) rational people do not believe that God exists, it is hardly self-evident that God exists. If belief in God is to be justified, such a belief must somehow be based upon observation or reason or both.[7]

Suppose that it could be demonstrated that Jack's belief in God is not consistent—that is, not even *possibly* true. If that were to happen, then in effect we would have shown that such a belief is not justified.[8] Inconsistent beliefs cannot be true. And it is hard to see how we can be justified in believing things that simply cannot be true.

1.6   Entrenchment and Tolerance

There are those who would argue that we do well to believe what other people believe and leave it at that. Quite obviously, this simplistic proposal has its problems. We might say that a belief is *entrenched* to the extent that it is shared by our contemporaries. Can we then assume that beliefs about the world are justified when and only when they are highly entrenched?

There is reason to doubt this. Consider a case where a small team of experts has made a strong but not conclusive case for a certain abstract hypothesis concerning DNA molecules. The hypothesis in question may then have every claim to being justified. But since very few people have heard of this hypothesis, it is not entrenched. It seems that entrenchment is not required for justification.

Arguably this works the other way as well. For example, as Paul M. Churchland has argued, it may be true that our "common-sense conception of heat" can be shown (by experts) to be "incoherent."[9] Highly entrenched beliefs concerning the nature of heat or temperature generally might turn out to be demonstrably inconsistent. If so, entrenchment does not guarantee justification. And if things work this way for "scientific" beliefs, why cannot things turn out the same way when we turn to metaphysical beliefs?

As we shall see in Chapter 2, some metaphysical systems are *revisionistic* in the sense that they conflict sharply with beliefs that most of us take for granted. Revisionary metaphysics is predicated upon the conviction that established or deeply entrenched accounts of what the world is like may be in need of extensive revision. I agree with the conviction in theory but think that a cautionary word is in order: voyages into revisionistic waters should not be undertaken lightly. Unless we are given good reasons for rejecting entrenched "commonsense" views concerning the world we inhabit, it is hard to see how we can be justified in abandoning such views.

It is, however, by no means clear that respect for common sense directs us to a unique metaphysical representation of the world we inhabit. Again the question arises whether there must be *one* correct way of viewing the world. It happens on occasion that different painters "see" the world in quite different but equally legitimate ways. We might also suspect that extraterrestrial beings and earthlings would see the world in quite different but equally legitimate ways. Perhaps the world, the universe we inhabit, is like a scene at a beach that lends itself to distinct but equally legitimate depictions or portrayals. If that is so, perhaps two observers of the cosmic stage might have different but equally respectable metaphysical systems. If so, perhaps arguments opposing or supporting various metaphysical systems reflect regrettable intolerance.

Undeniably, tolerance is often a good thing. But of course there can be too much of a good thing. If Jack and Jill, employing the same concepts, disagree when it comes to the question of the existence of ghosts or numbers, then it simply cannot be true that both ways of viewing the world are equally correct. It cannot be *true* both that supernatural beings exist and that supernatural beings do not exist, just as it cannot be true both that there is and is not a cat in the closet. In such cases we can hardly adopt a "One view is as good as another" approach to metaphysical issues. We cannot do this because both views simply *cannot* be true.

Can we know what the world is like? Is there even such a thing as "the way the world is" apart from the way we conceive of and conceptualize the world? Readers who incline toward metaphysical tolerance may suspect that this last question deserves a negative answer. Perhaps the best we can do is to describe as accurately as possible how people *think* about the world. When we try to go beyond this—try to say what the world is *really* like—we succeed merely in conveying more information concerning our own way of viewing the world. Or so it might be argued.

I think this is implausible. We are justified in believing that there are, really, tigers and teacups, foreign agents and fig trees. When we say that the world contains such things—that such things "exist"—we are not merely describing our way of thinking about the world. We are, rather, describing the way the world really is. Granted, this does not take us very far. We are still faced with all sorts of vexing questions concerning, say, supernatural beings and numbers and the nature of the mind. But it is at least a start. And why must things be different when we turn from teacups to prime numbers and supernatural beings? Why should questions about teacups have answers and questions about supernatural beings lack them?

The discussion that follows is based upon the assumption, succinctly stated by the contemporary American metaphysician Richard Taylor, that "[m]etaphysical questions have answers, and among competing answers, not all, certainly, can be true."[10] I grant that most of us find it hard to be certain what to say in response to many metaphysical questions. Truth can be a very elusive commodity in metaphysics, as in many other fields of inquiry. That is why it may be a good idea to emphasize metaphysical *respectability*. To determine whether a metaphysical position is "respectable," we must closely examine the arguments supporting and opposing it and, in light of this, decide whether, all things considered, the position is justified. For example, unless some convincing case can be made to support the view that God exists, this view fails to be metaphysically respectable. It takes little skill to *adopt* a metaphysical position. (One does this when one proclaims that numbers do not exist or that God does.) Skill *is* required of those who are intent upon arriving at a respectable position—a position that is both immune to serious objection and also supported by logical arguments based upon plausible and defensible premises. As we shall see, there are a great many proposals for explaining what the world is like. We cannot aspire to metaphysical respectability unless we are prepared to reflect seriously upon each question we encounter, doing our best to consider and weigh the merits of potential answers to such questions. It is not an undertaking for the fainthearted.

CHAPTER 2

*I*dealism

> *"Esse* is *percipi"* . . . asserts that "being" and "being experienced" are necessarily connected: that whatever *is* is *also* experienced. And this, I admit, cannot be directly refuted. But I believe it to be false. . . .
>
> G. E. MOORE, *PHILOSOPHICAL STUDIES* (1922)[1]

> The only thing whose existence we deny is that which philosophers call matter or corporeal substance. And in doing this there is no damage done to the rest of mankind, who, I dare say, will never miss it.
>
> GEORGE BERKELEY, *A TREATISE CONCERNING THE PRINCIPLES OF HUMAN KNOWLEDGE* (1710)[2]

2.1   Solipsism

Metaphysicians have a reputation, perhaps not entirely undeserved, for focusing attention upon abstract questions which, as critics charge, are far removed from the "real world" we encounter when we walk the dog or park the car. It is true that many abstract and difficult subjects fall within the province of metaphysics. What is not true is that metaphysics has little or no concern with commonplace things—things we encounter in our daily skirmishes with our immediate surroundings. The history of metaphysical thought is replete with examples of serious and even great thinkers struggling with metaphysical questions concerning the most familiar and ordinary objects. It is, however, true that the things metaphysicians have said about such objects sometimes conflict sharply with our ordinary way of viewing the world. Let us consider one example of such a metaphysical system.

Imagine a strange person—"Sol," we might call him—who is sitting in a large auditorium surrounded by hundreds of other people listening to a lecture. Sol sincerely *believes* that he is not in a lecture hall surrounded by other people. He is convinced, rather, that the lecturer, the audience, and the hall itself exist entirely in his own mind. If asked, Sol would be prepared to say sincerely that it *seems* to him "for all the world" *as if* he were really attending a lecture. But Sol insists that *appearances* can be misleading. Indeed, he believes that appearances are *systematically* misleading. What is really true, Sol believes, is that he presently is home in his bed *dreaming* that he is attending a lecture. Sol is prepared to grant that his dream is incredibly realistic. But he would, if asked, insist that it is nonetheless merely a dream—an experience depicting events that take place entirely in his own mind.

Sol would deny that the "chairs," "tables," and "human beings" that he "sees" are genuine substances. He believes that such things are mere ideas or images in his dream. But as I have described him, Sol does not believe that *all* putatively "material" things are really images or ideas in his mind. Since he *does* believe that he is really at home sleeping in his own bed, Sol would not be prepared to say that *his bed* is something that merely exists in his dream.

Consider a somewhat different case. Sol sincerely believes that *everything* that he "sees," "feels," or "perceives" is in reality a figment of his all-too-fertile imagination. In this case—though not in the former one—Sol accepts a position known as *solipsism*. As a solipsist, Sol believes that only he himself exists and that everything else is a mere figment of his incredibly lifelike or realistic dream.

2.2   A Painful Experience

I can *entertain* the solipsistic hypothesis that only I exist and that "everything else" is merely part of a rich and extended dream I am having. I reject this hypothesis as false. But do I *know* it is false? And if I do know this, precisely *how* do I know it? How do I know, for a start, that I am not now dreaming that I am sitting at a (genuine) desk typing on a (genuine) typewriter? The short answer is because I *see* the desk and the typewriter. Unhappily this short answer does not seem to settle the matter, since I often have the experience of "seeing" things in dreams.

The famous French philosopher René Descartes (1596–1650) was well aware of the problem:

> How often has it happened to me that in the night I dreamt that
> I found myself in this particular place, that I was dressed and
> seated by the fire, whilst in reality I was lying undressed in bed![3]

Descartes does not suggest that it is *true* that he is dreaming that he is sitting by a fire. His question concerns not truth but *knowledge*: How do I know that I am not now dreaming? I might ask a similar question with respect to the solipsistic hypothesis that only I exist and that *everything* else is part of my dream. How do I *know* that this hypothesis is false?

No doubt some people will be very impatient with this question. One of these people might approach me and proceed to step, deliberately and hard, on my toe. *"That's* no dream," he may assure me. In other words, he might conclude that I realize my solipsistic hypothesis is mistaken.

But of course this is hardly decisive. Following the lead of Descartes, I might reason as follows:

> How often has it happened that in the night I dreamt that I was
> standing on a street corner and that someone came up and
> stepped, very hard, on my toe whilst I was, in reality, lying
> undressed in bed!

This need not be taken to support the (false) view that the toe-stepping *really* occurs only in my dream. It might merely be cited in support of the more moderate—though perhaps equally mistaken— view that I do not really *know* that the toe-stepping occurs outside a dream, "in reality." Would I really know that you exist "in reality" and not "in my mind" if I were to have an experience in which you seemed to approach me and step on my toe?

2.3   The Case of the Prisoner and the Television Set

There is a good deal to be said concerning the conditions that must be satisfied if we are to *know* that something is true. Since this book's primary concern is not the subject of knowledge, either its nature or extent, I will not pursue this matter in any detail here. In the discussion that follows I will outline one famous argument suggesting that we can endorse the view that we know things about tables and chairs and mountains and trees (and so on) only if we are prepared to accept the revisionistic thesis that such things are *mind-*

dependent entities. If the argument is sound and we do indeed know things about tables and chairs and mountains and trees, we must radically revise our ordinary conception of tables and chairs and mountains and trees. Unless we are prepared to conclude that we know very little about the world in which we live, the argument suggests that we must accept a metaphysical position that is revisionistic in the extreme.

Try to imagine a person who is for some reason held prisoner in a small, bare, windowless room containing a television set. The prisoner spends most of her waking hours viewing the events and characters depicted on the screen. Understandably, she spends much time speculating as to what things are like outside the room she inhabits. Not surprisingly, she is inclined to believe that much of what she sees on her television screen represents or depicts "the real world" as it is outside her room. Tragically, she never is permitted to leave her room and so never is in a position to verify that the electronic "skyscrapers," "mountains," "horses," and other entities that she sees on her screen represent things that exist in reality. Our prisoner *believes* firmly that there really are such things as skyscrapers, mountains, and horses. (Indeed, her belief is true.) But does she *know* this? It is not hard to anticipate an argument supporting a negative answer to this question. Since the prisoner cannot get outside her room to verify that skyscrapers exist, she cannot be *certain* and so cannot know that such things exist.

This is, of course, a fanciful case, one that is unlikely ever to happen in fact. Still, some theorists would argue that the situation each of us is in is in some respects remarkably similar to that of the prisoner just described. Arguably, our *minds* are in some respects like television screens. Much as various objects may be pictured on a television screen, various things are pictured on the mental "screen" that is the mind. Just as *electronic* images exist on a television screen, *mental* images (ideas, sensations) exist on or in the mind. Some theorists go so far as to argue that each of us—each person—is only *immediately* or *directly* aware of the mental images on his or her private mental screen or mind. Thus Descartes says:

> I take the term "idea" to stand for whatever the mind is directly aware of.

When I perceive (see or feel) a table or a tree, I am directly or immediately aware of some "idea" that is in my mind—something that is located on my private mental screen. In the visual case, I believe that such ideas are produced by light waves that are reflected from a tree—a thing that exists off my mental screen, so to speak—and reflected to my eye. I conjecture that things work this way, but I am, strictly speaking, *directly* in touch with (directly aware of) only the idea, or tree image, that is located in my mind. We can no more step outside our minds to see what trees are *really* like than the prisoner can step outside her room in the hope of determining whether the electronic images she observes represent things that "really exist" outside her room.

If this model of the situation is correct, an impressive argument can be brought in support of *skepticism*—the view that we know little or nothing about tables, chairs, mountains, and horses. The argument is basically the same as the one considered earlier in the prisoner case. If I cannot step outside my mind and somehow find out what tables are really like, then I am never in a position to be certain that the images and ideas of tables in my mind (on my private mental screen) accurately *represent* things as they are *outside* my mind. And if I cannot be certain of this, then I *know* little or nothing about tables. Note that this argument is not designed to support solipsism. The argument under present consideration is directly concerned with knowledge and not with metaphysics. If sound, the argument suggests that while we may *believe* a great deal about tables and other entities, we in fact *know* very little about them.

Of course "common sense" assures us that we know a great deal about tables and chairs. But is common sense right about this? The problem arises when we consider the following propositions:

(A) Tables, chairs, trees, mountains, and so on exist outside the mind.

(B) We are immediately or directly aware only of things (ideas, sensations, thoughts, feelings) in the mind.

(C) We *know* and do not merely *believe* that there are tables, chairs, and so on. Indeed, we know a great deal about such things.

We may find it hard to see how all three propositions can be true. If we accept (A) and (B), we may find ourselves concluding that (C) is false. That is the conclusion of the skeptic.

But obviously this is not the only approach to the problem. We have two other options. First, we might hold that (C) and (B) are both true. So doing, we might proceed to argue that it is (A) that must be false. Advocates of this position are called *idealists*. Idealists argue that everything there is—everything that exists—is either a mind or something that exists in a mind. Contrary to (A), nothing exists outside the mind. Indeed, (A) must be rejected precisely *because* (B) and (C) are both true.

This line of argument presupposes that (A), (B), and (C) cannot *all* be true. But is that so? Our third option consists of showing that (B) and (C) do not pose a threat to (A). If we can do this, we will have taken a large step toward showing that neither skepticism nor idealism is well founded.

2.4   Berkeley's Independence Argument

Like Descartes, the English philosopher John Locke (1632–1704) held the view that many of the ideas *in* our minds represent things existing *outside* our minds. (More will be said about Locke in Chapter 4.) This representational model of the situation has undeniable appeal. Nonetheless, the representational model was challenged by the Irish philosopher George Berkeley (1685–1753). On the standard interpretation of his position, it appeared to Berkeley:

> . . . that Locke's picture of the world embodied an absurd and quite needless *duplication*. There are, first of all, the things that we actually perceive, which Locke calls "ideas"; and then, Locke adds, there are behind or beyond the ideas completely unobservable counterparts, which he regards as the real physical objects.[4]

Followers of Locke and Descartes often speak of people *seeing* and *feeling* things such as trees and tables. But their theory of perception seems to imply that one is not directly aware of the "external" things one is said to "see" or "feel." (One is directly aware of things in the mind—ideas—that represent what is said to exist outside the mind.) Berkeley regarded the hypothesis of "external" objects—objects existing outside the mind—as "the very root of skepticism":

> . . . for so long as men thought that real things subsisted without the mind, and that their knowledge was only so forth *real* as it was conformable to *real things,* it follows that they could not be

certain they had any real knowledge at all. For how can it be known that the things which are perceived are conformable to those which are not perceived or exist without the mind?

There is reason to believe that Berkeley associated *material* or *corporeal* substance with Locke's unknown and unknowable "something I know not what" that bears or supports qualities. Rejecting mysterious Lockean substances, Berkeley himself subscribed to a bundle theory according to which an ordinary thing (a tree, say) is nothing more than a collection of qualities. Since qualities are for Berkeley mind-dependent entities, ordinary things are mind-dependent entities.

Berkeley's arguments are very subtle and interesting, and I cannot and will not try to do them justice here. The *general* proposal is, however, simple: we can avoid skepticism—can establish a case for judging that we do indeed know many things concerning tables and mountains and so on—only if we allow that we are *directly* and *immediately* aware of such things when we see and feel them. Since we can only be directly aware of *ideas,* Berkeley concludes that tables and mountains are ideas, or, more precisely, collections of ideas. It is important to recognize that Berkeley does not argue that we live in a world *lacking* tables, mountains, lakes, and so on. Berkeley is no solipsist. On the contrary, he believes that such things are perfectly real. The surprising thesis for which Berkeley argues concerns the true *nature* of such commonplace things. Berkeley is no skeptic when it comes to claims of knowledge about commonplace things. Indeed, it is precisely because we *have* knowledge of such things that Berkeley believes we should conclude that these entities are really collections of ideas.

Berkeley is an idealist, but he is no solipsist. The ideas that make up the world of commonplace things are, he argues, *independent* of his mind or will. However, since every idea is mind-dependent, Berkeley concludes that his mind is not the only mind there is:

> When in broad daylight I open my eyes, it is not in my power to choose whether I shall see or no, or to determine what particular objects shall present themselves to my view; and so likewise as to the hearing and other senses; the ideas imprinted on them are not creatures of my will. There is therefore some *other* spirit that produces them.[5]

I have reason to believe that I am not the only sentient being in existence since (1) many of the ideas in my mind come from outside my mind and (2) such ideas can only be produced by some mind (spirit) other than my own. Berkeley proceeds to argue that no finite, human mind could be responsible for my perceptual ideas. Only an *infinite* spirit could do the job. Berkeley calls this infinite spirit "God":

> Among spirits there is one infinite spirit, God; and there are many finite spirits, men among them. . . . Finite minds have small power to cause ideas; but when we observe the world around us, we are for ever being affected with the ideas that God's mind perceives, and which by God's will finite spirits also perceive.[6]

At present I see a certain oak tree. What sort of thing is it I see? If we say that the tree exists outside the mind, Berkeley thinks we will be unable to defend the commonsense view that we *know* various things about the tree. Suppose, on the other hand, that the tree exists *in* the mind. This allows us to say that the tree is knowable, but it implies—since only ideas exist in the mind—that the tree is a collection of ideas. Critics may charge that this simply cannot be true, since no collection of ideas persists or endures—continues to exist—in the way that the tree persists or endures. Presumably I do not have any ideas when I am in a sound sleep. If the tree I presently see is a collection of ideas, it is hard to see how the tree can exist when I am sleeping soundly. Berkeley anticipated this objection to his position and believed that he had a good reply to it. The tree persists or endures when no human being, no finite spirit, is perceiving or thinking of it. No collection of ideas in any finite mind can correctly be identified with the tree. Since—as Berkeley thought he had demonstrated—the tree *is* a collection of ideas and every collection of ideas must exist in *some* mind, the tree must exist in an *infinite* mind or spirit. In short, Berkeley concluded that the persistence of the tree gives us good reason to conclude that there exists an *infinite* spirit, God. What other hypothesis could possibly account for the fact that the tree—a collection of ideas—continues to exist even at times when no finite spirit or ordinary person perceives the tree? No collection of ideas is mind-independent. Since the tree I presently see is a collection of ideas and is independent of finite spirits, it follows that there must be an infinite spirit (mind) upon which the tree depends for its continued existence.

2.5   Frege's Objection

Because Berkeley's metaphysical position relies so heavily on God's pervasive and constant activity, a natural way to challenge his position is to dispute the thesis that God exists. Later, in Chapter 11, I will have more to say concerning the question of God's existence. Here it is important to note that Berkeley's idealism can be challenged *without* disputing the existence of God. The great German logician Gottlob Frege (1848–1925) presses an objection that is independent of the claim that God does not exist. To see how Frege's challenge proceeds, let us focus attention upon two "finite spirits": Jack and Jill. Each individual has thoughts, feelings, and memories and each also perceives various ideas. Can Jack and Jill perceive *the same idea*? Suppose that Jack has a headache and Jill has a headache as well. Here we may well deny that Jack and Jill feel, or "perceive," *the same thing*. Jack feels *Jack's* headache, Jill feels *Jill's* headache. Jack does not feel *Jill's* headache, nor does Jill feel *Jack's* headache. More generally, each of us perceives (feels) his or her own agony and, on occasion, ecstasy. If things work the same way for "ideas" generally, then each of us perceives his or her own ideas. This model of the situation is reinforced when we consider the apparent fact that my ideas are accessible to me in some direct way that the ideas of other spirits are not. Frege saw the situation this way:

> It is so much the essence of each of my ideas to be the content of my consciousness, that every idea of every other person is, just as such, distinct from mine. But might it not be possible that my ideas, the entire content of my consciousness, might be at the same time the content of a more embracing, perhaps divine, consciousness? Only if I were myself part of the divine consciousness. But then would they really be my ideas, would I be their bearer?

If Frege's hypothesis is correct, it poses any number of problems for followers of Berkeley. For suppose that various ideas in Jack's mind are not merely similar to but strictly the same as (identical with) ideas in God's mind. If Frege is right, this means that Jack's mind (consciousness) must then be *part of the divine consciousness.* But is this possible? Can each finite spirit, so to speak, be part of the divine spirit (God)? Suppose that Jack plans—in the manner of Dostoyevsky's character Raskolnikov in *Crime and Punishment*—to rob and then murder a helpless old woman. Since Jack has an "evil mind," it then follows—assuming that Jack's mind is part of God's mind—that *God* has an evil mind. This result conflicts sharply with the view that God is essentially good.[7] If we think that there is indeed a God who is essentially good, then I suspect we shall be hard pressed to defend the view that each of our minds is somehow part of God's mind.

But perhaps the main problem arises when we set assumptions concerning morality to one side. If we are told that Lake Michigan, say, is in reality a collection of ideas, then we may well ask "Whose ideas?" Frege's hypothesis is that no single idea is ever located in two or more minds. (Of course, two people may each have the same sort of idea, just as two people may each have the same sort of pain. But one pain cannot be felt by two people, nor can one idea be thought by two people.) If Frege is right about this, then it seems that no *collection* of ideas is ever located in two or more minds. The problem this poses for Berkeley and his followers is obvious: if Lake Michigan is identified with some collection of ideas in *my* mind, then Lake Michigan simply cannot also be identified with any collection of ideas in *your* mind. Assuming that you are directly aware only of ideas in your mind, it then follows—contrary to what Berkeley believes—that you and other finite spirits generally cannot be directly aware of Lake Michigan. Lake Michigan exists in *my mind* if Lake Michigan is a collection of *my* ideas and if, also, Frege's hypothesis (that different minds cannot have literally the same ideas) is correct.

How should idealists respond to this? I suppose that they might, in desperation, reply by denying that there is a *single* Lake Michigan. Your Lake Michigan consists of a certain collection of ideas in *your* mind, my Lake Michigan consists of a certain collection of ideas in *my* mind, and so on. On this strange view, there are as many Lake Michigans as there are finite spirits "perceiving" Lake Michigan. It seems that each finite spirit, each *person,* has his or her own private world populated by his or her "own" Lake Michigan, Eiffel Tower, Atlantic Ocean, and so on. It seems that there simply is no such thing as *the world.* Each finite spirit has his or her *own* private world populated by his or her own lakes, rivers, trees, and so on. Such is one version of idealism without solipsism.

I suspect that Frege would have been a bit impatient with this metaphysical position. Surely there is one and only one Lake Michigan, Eiffel Tower, Atlantic Ocean, and so on. Frege might have argued that this plain fact strongly suggests if it does not actually show that no version of the idealist's story can possibly be correct. If the lake I see when I see Lake Michigan is a collection of ideas in my mind and the lake you see when you see Lake Michigan is a collection of ideas in your mind, then—assuming Frege's hypothesis that the same ideas cannot be located in different minds—your lake and my lake must be different lakes. But common sense says that in certain circumstances *we see the same lake*.

2.6   Lost Virtue

Of course it may be objected that all of this ignores the possibility that the "real" Lake Michigan is a collection of ideas in *God's* mind. This move has obvious attractions for the idealist:

> Since God's perception is not fragmented by time or distributed across different minds, the physical world perceived has the requisite unity: it is not a collection of isolated ideas, but one complex idea, which contains all physical items in a single spatio-temporal field. Likewise, since God's perception is not subject to the limitations of human perception, the physical world can be as extensive and replete as we ordinarily believe: there is no problem in supposing that there were mountains and rivers before there were humans to perceive them or that my desk continues to exist when there is no one in my room.[8]

Unhappily there is a high price to be paid if this position is adopted. One of the alleged virtues of an idealist analysis of ordinary things such as trees and mountains is that it enables us to reject the problematic "representational" view of Descartes and Locke, according to which we are never *directly aware* of trees and mountains (but only of ideas or sensations representing trees and mountains). But *this supposed virtue is lost* if trees and mountains are identified with collections of ideas in *God's* mind. It seems that my ideas, located in my mind, at best *represent* or somehow depict the trees and mountains that exist in God's mind. Presumably if I have no "direct access" to the contents of your mind, then neither do I have direct access to the contents of God's mind. The problem is that

> . . . by locating the physical world in God's mind, Berkeley is now committed to saying that our access to it is only indirect. We perceive physical objects, but only by perceiving certain other objects, i.e., our own ideas, which represent them.[9]

All the problems concerning *knowledge* which idealism was supposed to resolve now emerge with a vengeance. If Jack's ideas are said to represent the real Lake Michigan—allegedly a collection of ideas in God's mind—then how can Jack or any other finite spirit know for sure that what does the representing is an accurate portrayal of what is represented? Presumably no finite spirit has "direct access" to the contents of God's mind. So if the universe is itself located in God's mind, it seems that we have no direct access to the universe. Unless knowledge is possible without direct access, it may be charged that Berkeley is faced with precisely the same problem concerning knowledge as are Descartes and Locke. The proclaimed virtue of idealism was that it could solve this problem. But this supposed virtue may appear illusory if the universe is said to be located in God's mind.

2.7   Kripke's Thesis

Is it not theoretically *possible* that the tree outside my window—and commonplace things generally—are collections of divine ideas? Our initial reaction might be that the question deserves an affirmative answer. But recent work done by Saul Kripke, a philosopher at Princeton University, suggests that this first reaction may be mistaken. Consider what Kripke says about water:

> It certainly represents a discovery that water is H_2O. We identified water originally by its characteristic feel, appearance and perhaps taste. . . . If there were a substance, even actually, which had a completely different atomic structure from that of water, but resembled water in these respects, would we say that some water wasn't H_2O? I think not. We would say instead that just as there was fool's gold there could be fool's water. . . .[10]

Perhaps we can apply Kripke's reasoning to the hypothesis that it *might* be true that water is a collection of ideas in God's mind (and by implication the hypothesis that it might be true that my tree is such a collection of ideas). Kripke would allow that it might happen that stuff that was not really a compound of hydrogen and oxygen *looked*, for all the world, *like* water. What he denies is that such stuff would *be* genuine water. Kripke defends the following thesis:

> **(K)** If (genuine) water is in fact a compound of hydrogen and oxygen, then it is necessarily true that (genuine) water is a compound of hydrogen and oxygen.

Conjoining (K) and (1):

> **(1)** In fact, genuine water is a compound of hydrogen and oxygen.

gives the result, in (2), that:

> **(2)** It is necessarily true (and not "contingently" true) that water is a compound of hydrogen and oxygen.

Assuming further that no compound of hydrogen and oxygen is a collection of ideas, it seems to follow, in (3), that:

> **(3)** It is necessarily true (and not "contingently" true) that water is not a collection of ideas.

If this is right, it is not even *possibly true*—much less actually true—that water is a collection of ideas in or out of God's mind. What is possible, perhaps, is that some collection of ideas in God's mind *appears,* for all the world, to be water. We might mistakenly judge that we were confronted by genuine water when in fact we are confronted by such a collection of divine ideas. If Kripke is right, however, this does not show that genuine water might be a collection of ideas in God's mind. What it does show is, at most, that we might encounter stuff that looked for all the world *like* water and that nonetheless was a collection of divine ideas. Such stuff would not be genuine water, but only "fool's water." The point can be extended, in an obvious way, to challenge the thesis that the tree outside my window might be, even if in fact it is not, a collection of divine ideas. If the treelike object located outside my window is made of cardboard or plastic, what I see is a *fool's* tree and not a *genuine* tree. (Similarly if the object I see is composed of ideas in God's mind.) If Kripke is right—and I am inclined to think he is—there is no real possibility that a genuine glass of water or a genuine tree is in reality a collection of ideas in any mind. We may doubt that Berkeley's idealist analysis of such things is even possibly true or *consistent*. And metaphysical views that are demonstrably not consistent fail to be respectable.

Of course it may be said that it is *possible*, *for all we know*, that commonplace things such as trees and glasses of water are collections of ideas in God's mind. Let us grant this, for the sake of argument, and see what follows. Does it follow that it is *really* possible that the treelike object I presently see outside my window is a collection of ideas in God's mind?

Not if Kripke is right. To see why, consider a case in which a tribe of primitive people encounter a body of genuine water. These people do not *know* that the water is made up of H_2O molecules. So it is *possible*, *for all they know*, that the water they encounter is made up of something other than H_2O molecules. This does not license the conclusion that it is *really* possible that the stuff encountered is made up of something other than H_2O molecules. Since the stuff encountered is—as we assume—genuine water, Kripke's arguments suggest that this stuff really could not be composed of anything other than H_2O molecules. The "possibility" that the stuff encountered might be composed of something else reflects at best the ignorance of the primitive people. In reality, things could not be the way things "might be" for all these people know.

2.8 A Challenge

I am inclined to think that we know very well that trees and glasses of water are not made up of ideas in any mind. But I shall not try to defend this conviction here. The important thing is that none of Berkeley's arguments gives us really good reasons for subscribing to the idealist thesis that everything there is either is a mind (spirit) or an idea (collection of ideas). Of course, I have not addressed all Berkeley's arguments in this necessarily brief discussion.

Some theorists are prepared to grant Berkeley at least a partial victory. In a paper entitled "Berkeley on the Physical World," John Foster, a contemporary philosopher working at Oxford University, says:

> Where I think [Berkeley] goes seriously wrong is in assuming that the conclusion of [his] reasoning is enough to vindicate the mentalist doctrine. What the reasoning establishes is that if the

ultimate ontology is not confined to minds and ideas, the additional entities are ones of whose intrinsic natures we can form no positive conception. But it by no means follows from this that there are no such entities or even that it would be irrational to postulate them.[11]

In a sense, Foster here poses a challenge to the view, which I suspect will be widely shared, that it is true both that (A) Berkeley's idealist analysis of commonplace "material" things is mistaken or at least unfounded and (B) we know very well what the intrinsic nature of such things is. If we subscribe to (A) and (B), we owe Foster an alternative to Berkeley's idealist analysis of "material" objects. In Chapters 4 through 6, we shall consider a number of competing accounts of material things. First, however, let us turn attention to the *mind*. It seems that you and I have minds, while mountains and trees do not. The question is precisely what *is* a mind?

CHAPTER 3

Material Minds

... the mind is simply the central nervous system, or, less accurately but more epigrammatically, the mind is simply the brain.
DAVID ARMSTRONG, *A MATERIALIST THEORY OF MIND* (1968)[1]

3.1 Elizabeth's Question

Most of us have misgivings concerning Berkeley's view that rivers and mountains are collections of ideas existing in the mind. We may agree that matter cannot be reduced to mind—agree also that material things are not dependent upon the existence of any mind—and still disagree when it comes to this fundamental question:

What sort of thing is the mind?

The mind is a first-class troublemaker, metaphysically speaking. Presumably there is a sense in which each of us knows his or her own mind. Each of us knows, perhaps in some direct or privileged way, things about what we believe and desire. Perhaps it is the conviction that a person has privileged access to her mind that accounts, at least in part, for the appeal of the hypothesis that our minds are not material substances. Most of us know very little, if anything, about the object that is our brain. One can know a good deal about one's mind and also know almost nothing about one's brain. This apparent fact encourages the conviction that our minds cannot be material substances. If my mind were a material substance, presumably my mind would be my brain. But identity requires indiscernibility. How can my mind be my brain when I know a great many things about my mind even though I do not know very much about my brain?

This is the sort of reasoning that leads people to endorse the metaphysical position called *dualism.* Dualists argue that the world contains material substances such as our bodies and also immaterial substances called "minds."

> A Dualist theory is one that holds that mind and body are *distinct things.* For a Dualist a man is a compound object, a material thing—his body—somehow related to a non-material thing or things—his mind.[2]

In a sense, the term "dualist" is misleading, since dualists might argue that the world contains many "composite" things that cannot properly be said to be either entirely "material" or entirely "immaterial." Dualists may reject the view that the world contains only two fundamental kinds of things—material substances and immaterial substances. They may argue instead that the world contains *three* kinds of things, namely, material substances such as human bodies, immaterial substances such as our minds, and composite things made up of at least one material substance and one immaterial substance. Arguably you and I are in the composite category. Conceivably you are a composite entity made up of a certain material substance (your body) and also of a certain immaterial substance (your mind).[3] Why not?

There is no denying that dualism has its attractions. But we should not endorse dualism without appreciating the potential problems that arise for the view that minds are not material things. One such problem emerges in a famous letter written to Descartes by Princess Elizabeth in 1643.[4]

> . . . I beg of you to tell me how the human soul can determine the movement of the animal spirits in the body so as to perform voluntary acts. . . . For the determination of movement seems always to come about from the moving body's being propelled—to depend on the kind of impulse it gets from what sets it in motion . . . and contact seems to me incompatible with a thing's being immaterial.[5]

Elizabeth is questioning the suggestion, made by Descartes, that an immaterial mind is capable of producing results in a material substance such as a human body. How can something that is *not* composed of matter bring about movement, say, on the part of something that is composed of matter? Many contemporary philosophers judge that the question raises serious or even fatal problems for dualists.[6] Indeed, Elizabeth's question might easily be turned into an argument opposing dualism.

3.2   An Argument from Causality

Suppose that your mind were an immaterial substance. Could it then produce movements involving your arms, legs, and other bodily parts? This is Princess Elizabeth's problem. Elizabeth conjectures that one thing can move another only if the first thing comes into *contact* with the second thing. But how can an immaterial substance come into contact with a material thing such as an arm or leg? If the production of movement requires contact and contact is impossible between immaterial and material things, then, Elizabeth reasons, immaterial things cannot produce movement in material things. Either the mind is—as opposed to the view of Descartes—a material thing *or* it does not produce movement in the various parts of the body.

Let us say that x is a *proper part* of y if and only if (1) x is part of y and (2) there is something other than x—let us call it z—such that z is a part of y. There is then apparent reason to judge that your mind is a proper part of you. Obviously your *nose* is not your *mind*. Your nose is one part of you and your mind is still another part. Thus your mind is a proper part of you. But which part, exactly?

What assures us that your nose is not your mind? The answer might be said to lie in the fact that your nose does not have thoughts, memories, desires, or plans. Unlike your *mind,* your nose does not deliberate—does not make decisions and subsequently act to carry out these decisions. We might judge that a person's *mind* is that proper part of a person that in normal circumstances is apt to produce or bring about deliberate or intentional behavior. Since a person's nose has no plausible claim to performing such a function, there is simply no basis for identifying noses with minds.

On this view of things, the essence of the mind is specified in terms of a certain causal role: whatever part of a person typically produces, in normal circumstances, deliberative behavior thereby qualifies as this person's mind. Suppose, for example, that Jack deliberately and intentionally insults Jill. Clearly the movement of Jack's lips, which utter the words conveying the insult to Jill, is produced by certain of his *beliefs* and *desires.* Since beliefs and desires are psychological states and psychological states are states of a person's mind, the movement of the lips is somehow brought about by Jack's mind. The crucial question is whether there is some immaterial part of a person that fills the appropriate causal role and so qualifies as the mind. Materialists deny this.

> [T]he causal theory of the mind does lead naturally on to a materialist theory of the mind. For suppose that we consider all the outward physical behavior of human beings, and other higher animals, which we take to be mind-betokening. In the light of current knowledge, it seems quite likely that the *sole* causes of this behavior are external physical stimuli together with internal physiological processes, in particular physiological processes in the central nervous system. But if we accept this premise on grounds of general scientific plausibility, and also accept the causal theory of the mind, the mental must in fact be physiological.[7]

In simplified form, the causal argument in behalf of a materialist analysis of mind proceeds along these lines:

(1) A person's mind is that (proper) part of the person that normally produces or brings about this person's deliberative behavior.

(2) Scientific research reveals that it is physiological activity in a person's brain that normally produces or brings about this person's deliberative behavior.

Therefore

(3) A person's mind is his or her brain.

It certainly seems that your brain qualifies as a material substance. So if your mind is indeed your brain, your *mind* is a material substance. States of mind are, accordingly, states of a certain material object. Assuming that anger is a state of mind, it seems that the state of anger is a certain material state of the brain of the person who is angry. The essence of anger is that it is an inner state of a person that typically produces—is "apt" to produce in normal circumstances—a certain range of "anger" behavior.

Materialists believe that "general scientific" experimental results will indicate that certain physiological, electrical, and chemical states of a person's brain turn out to play the causal role that is definitive of anger. Such internal physical states are themselves typically caused by various external physical stimuli—perhaps sound waves impinging upon a person's ears and conveying an insult or nasty remark. The essence of each mental state is similarly defined in terms of a certain typical causal role that results in certain sorts of behavior. The essence of anger is quite different from the essence of contentment, since the former state typically produces behavior that is quite different from that of the latter. But in both cases it turns out that states of the brain play the causal role that is definitive of the mind. This suggests that the brain *is* the mind—is, indeed, identical with it. Since the brain obviously is a material substance, it follows that the mind is a material substance.

3.3   A Phenomenological Objection

Of course not everyone views the mind in this light. Some critics argue that the causal analysis of mental states defended by materialists is mistaken. Consider a fiendish professor of psychology who rewires the physiological circuits of Alice's brain in such a way that the following happens:

(A) Whenever Alice's brain is in physiological state S this prompts Alice to display aggressive behavior toward others, to say harsh things in a loud voice, to shake her fists, get red in the face, to tremble as if "in rage," and so on.

(B) Alice *feels* nothing at all when she is in state S.

In light of (A), it seems that state S should qualify as genuine *anger* if the causal analysis of anger is correct. But (B) may suggest that state S is not genuine anger at all. How can it happen that a person who feels nothing at all feels *angry*? Judging this to be impossible, critics reject the causal analysis of anger. Extending the argument, we might question the "causal analysis" of mind proposed by materialists. Our fiendish professor might, in theory, arrange things so that Alice never *felt* anything but nonetheless behaved as other people behave. Alice cries when insulted (but feels nothing), laughs when told a good joke (but feels nothing), . . . and so on. Here we may judge that Alice *lacks a mind* entirely. Alice is "programmed," in an incredibly ingenious way, to behave *as if* she had a mind. Since the causal analysis of mind upon which materialism rests implies (falsely) that Alice has a mind, the causal analysis of mind must accordingly be rejected.

Critics who press this objection insist that the essence of anger (pain, hunger, love, hatred, jealousy, etc.) is that it *feels* a certain way "from the inside." Thomas Nagel is driving at this point when he observes that:

> [W]e believe that bats feel some version of pain, fear, hunger, and lust, and that they have other, more familiar types of perception beside sonar. But we believe that these experiences also have in each case a specific subjective character, which it is beyond our ability to conceive.[8]

We humans cannot know very much about what it is like to be a bat or a snake. But presumably we can know a good deal about what it is like to be a human being. The study of what this is like "from the inside" might be called *human phenomenology*. If those of us who are not bats cannot understand much about bat phenomenology, then perhaps individuals who are not human cannot understand much about human phenomenology. Why is this? One possible answer is that nonbats cannot *feel* or *experience* the things bats feel, and nonhuman cannot feel or experience many of the things humans feel or experience. Contrary to what materialists tell us, perhaps the *essence* of human anger is that it *feels* a certain way. Internal states that lack the appropriate "feel" fail to qualify as states of genuine anger, even if such states produce behavior of the sort normally produced by genuine anger. The causal argument in behalf of materialism fails because it rests upon a mistaken analysis of mental states such as anger and happiness.

3.4   Private Languages

We may expect materialists to make a spirited (so to speak) defense of their position. Consider the case of the fiendish professor. Materialists will agree that state S is not genuine anger. Genuine anger is an internal state that *normally* produces a certain typical behavior. But it does not normally happen that states of type S produce such behavior. Alice's case is exceptional. Those of us who have not been subjected to the fiendish professor's "rewiring" experiment are in a quite different internal state—are not in state S—when we normally exhibit angry behavior. Thus materialists are not committed to judging, falsely, that state S is genuine anger. State S simply is not a state that normally fills the causal role which is definitive of anger.

Materialists may also argue that it is a mistake to judge that mental or psychological states are properly defined in terms of their subjective character, the way they feel "from the inside." Suppose that someone makes an especially insulting remark and thereby causes me to be angry. Suppose further that I were to *define* "anger" as meaning "internal state that feels like *this.*" Could I then ever *know* that other people were angry? I cannot "get inside" another person's mind, cannot verify in any direct way that other people who are red in the face and shaking their fists feel what I feel when I refer to my "internal state that feels like *this.*" Given my definition of anger, it seems I can never *know* that another person *is* angry. But on reflection, this seems silly. I know very well that my friend John was angry when he spilled his soup on his expensive rug last week. Materialists may argue that this fact—that one person sometimes knows when other people are angry (happy, hungry, jealous)—conflicts with the claim that mental states are properly defined "from the inside" in terms of the subjective character of certain experiences. In fact, each of us knows many things about what goes on in *other minds.* Such knowledge would be impossible if the essence of the mind and its states were properly analyzed in terms of subjective character. Materialists conclude that only a causal analysis of the mind will accommodate the fact that we have knowledge of other minds.[9]

The materialists' counterattack might be posed in somewhat different terms. Imagine the following cruel technique of language acquisition: At some stage in their education, children are told to place their hands on a table. The children's hands are then struck sharply with a ruler, whereupon they are told "What you presently feel is *pain.*" Emerging from this traumatic encounter, each child takes the word "pain" to mean "sensation of the sort I felt when struck on the hands with a ruler." Here it might appear that the subjective "phenomenological" character of a certain sensation or experience is definitive of what the word "pain" means. However, materialists may well challenge this model of things. One person can never feel, and so can never be directly acquainted with, the sensation experienced by another person. Accordingly it seems that if "pain" is defined in terms of the subjective character of inner experiences, then each speaker must have his or her *private* definition of what the word "pain" means. There is simply no way of *checking* to ensure that what one speaker means by the word "pain" is the same as what others mean by it, on the present model. But this is fishy. Critics argue that something is seriously wrong with the present model of the mind. Arguably words such as "pain" and "anger," and indeed all words in natural languages such as English, are employed in accordance with *public* rules—rules whose observance or violation is subject to public scrutiny or verification.[10] Since words in natural or public languages cannot—if we are to avoid linguistic anarchy—be defined privately, terms such as "pain" cannot be defined in terms of the subjective character of what speakers feel when struck with rulers. Therefore the phenomenological features of mental states are not definitive of these states. (If they were, none of us could know that we were employing terms such as "pain" and "joy" in the way other people employ these terms.) The phenomenological argument opposing materialism that was outlined in section 3.3 thus fails.

3.5   Epiphenomenalism

In theory, we might reject the proposal that mental terms can be defined "from the inside," so to speak; we might *also* have misgivings concerning the causal argument in behalf of materialism that was presented in section 3.2. Suppose that I desperately want a glass of milk and accordingly open the door of the refrigerator and take out the milk. Does my strong desire for milk *really* cause the movements of my body when this happens? In an interesting paper entitled "Psychology as Philosophy," Donald Davidson argues that causation works according to laws:

> [W]hen events are related as cause and effect, then there exists
> a closed and deterministic system of laws into which these
> events, when appropriately described, fit.[11]

If Davidson is right about this, then my desire for milk causes the event wherein my hand opens the refrigerator door *only on the condition* that it is true that there is a lawlike relation between such desire-events and such door-opening events. But *is* there really such a law? (And exactly what is a law?) Standard "natural" laws such as the laws of thermodynamics and the law of gravity do not appear to correlate *psychological* events and physical events. Agreeing with this, Davidson would argue further that "there are no precise psychophysical laws." All this might be thought to present a formidable challenge to the causal theory of the mind considered earlier. How can the mind be causally responsible for many things the body does if indeed causality requires lawlike regularities and there are no psychophysical laws?

Is it conceivable that the mind is *not* causally related to the various movements of our bodies? Some theorists—they are called *epiphenomenalists*—argue that this is indeed the way things work. (Davidson himself is not an epiphenomenalist, for reasons that will emerge shortly.) Epiphenomenalists deny that psychological events and states can properly be identified with material events and states. Certain chemical and electrical events in our nervous systems produce psychological events such as desires; they also produce bodily movements—the movements of my hand when it opens the door of the refrigerator, for example. As Princess Elizabeth suspected, every bodily movement is produced by a physical cause—an electrical or chemical event within the nervous system that may also produce psychological events such as a desire to drink milk. The fact that a strong desire to drink milk is in many cases correlated with bodily movements involving the drinking of milk suggests that such a desire causes drinking-of-milk bodily movements. But this appearance is deceptive, since the bodily movements in question have physical causes and since desires—and other psychological events—are not physical events. In the milk case, the accompanying diagram represents roughly the epiphenomenalist assessment of the situation.

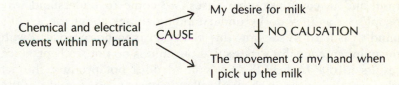

When generalized, this model appears to be consistent with a dualist assessment, that our minds are immaterial substances and our bodies material substances. Psychological activity and psychological events occur in the mind, while physiological (electrical and chemical) events occur in the body. Since there are no psychological-physical laws linking psychological events or psychological states such as desires with movements of our bodies, and since causality requires that there be such laws, psychological events and psychological states do not produce or cause movements of our bodies. Thus the causal argument supporting a materialist analysis of mind that was considered earlier (section 3.2) is unsound. This argument fails because it falsely assumes that a person's mind is that part of the person that typically produces or causes intentional behavior. What is true, our epiphenomenalist argues, is that behavior—movements of bodies and parts of bodies—is produced by physical activity within human brains (more generally, activity within the human nervous system). Since minds do not in fact cause behavior, it is a mistake to analyze the mind as that which typically produces behavior. Accordingly, we are not entitled to conclude from the fact that behavior is typically produced by the brain that our minds can properly be identified with our brains.

3.6   Davidson's Materialism

Should we embrace epiphenomenalism? I think not. For one thing, epiphenomenalists are committed to the claim that all human behavior—every action that a person performs—is in theory explainable without reference to the mind or the mental states of the person who is the agent. But this claim is very implausible. What explains the fact that Alice is presently taking her umbrella out of the closet? Alice does this because (1) she believes that it is likely to rain today and (2) she desires to remain dry if it does rain. Note that the operative terms "believes" and "desires" both concern Alice's *psychological* states—if you will, states of Alice's mind. In this case, and in countless other cases, we come to understand why people act as they do by understanding things about the agent's mind. It is hard to see how this plain fact is to be reconciled with the epiphenomenalist's thesis that our minds do not really produce results in our bodies. If Alice's mind does not produce the act wherein Alice picks up the umbrella, then what can we make of the "because" in the statement "Alice picks up the umbrella because she believes it will rain"?

Epiphenomenalists also face worries concerning responsibility. Most of us believe that the tightening of the killer's finger on the trigger is caused by a decision made by the killer. Since the decision is a "mental" event that takes place in the mind of the killer, we believe that mental events (events in the mind) cause bodily actions. Epiphenomenalists argue that this view of the matter is mistaken and that the pulling of the trigger is an event brought about by some nonmental physiological or neural activity within the killer's body. However, it is hard to see how this account is to be reconciled with the fact, as I take it to be, that killers are often *responsible* for their actions. The conviction that people are responsible for their actions is closely tied to the commonsense view that many actions are "intentional" in the sense (roughly) that these actions are brought about by *decisions* and *choices* on the part of the agent. But presumably decision-making activity qualifies as *mental* activity if anything does. This suggests that the very fact that people are responsible for their actions gives us reason to distrust the epiphenomenalist's claim that minds do not cause behavior.[12]

Contrary to epiphenomenalists, I believe there is reason to judge that my *decision* to go to the refrigerator and get the milk plays a central role in the production of the movements of my hand as it lifts the milk from the refrigerator. It is simply not true that psychological events never cause bodily movements. Davidson agrees with this, arguing that "psychological events . . . are directly or indirectly caused by, and causes of, physical events." If Davidson is right—and here I think he is—we must reject the epiphenomenalist's thesis that the mind is causally impotent when it comes to producing bodily movements. But we are left with a problem. Davidson endorses each of the following propositions:

(1) Psychological events cause physical events (bodily movements).
(2) Causality requires laws. Events that are causally related are linked by a lawlike tie or connection.
(3) There are no psychophysical laws. (For example, there is no physical law that says that strong desires for milk are followed by movements wherein our hands bring milk to our lips.)

We might judge that these propositions are inconsistent—that all three propositions simply *cannot* be true. Indeed, epiphenomenalists might argue that Davidson is right about (2) and (3) and so conclude that Davidson is mistaken about (1). But as we have just seen, there is reason to doubt that epiphenomenalists are right in rejecting (1). Indeed, Davidson would argue that (1), (2), and (3) are all true. The three propositions can be jointly true only because "psychological events are describable, taken one by one, in physical terms." When we speak in psychological terms of "desires," "fears," and "pains," we cannot formulate any lawlike connection between our minds and the movements of our bodies. But perhaps things work out differently if desires, fears, and pains are described in terms of a person's electrical and chemical states. When the mind is described in *physical* terms, perhaps there are lawlike connections between things that happen in our mind and actions such as picking up an umbrella or pulling the trigger of a gun.

The heart of Davidson's position is that we have very good reason to conclude that our minds can, in theory, be described in physical terms. Therefore, says Davidson, we have reason to reject the idea that our minds are immaterial things. In the normal course of things, our minds *do* cause movements of our bodies. Since causality requires lawlike connections between causes and effects, Davidson concludes that it must in theory be possible to describe the mind—to describe desires, pains, and beliefs—in terms that allow for lawlike connections between what happens in the mind and movements of the body. Only a *physical* (electrical and chemical) description of the mind will provide the basis for establishing law-like connections between mental events and their physical causes. Therefore our minds must be describable in physical terms. Since no immaterial object is describable in physical terms, we can conclude that our minds are not immaterial objects.

Thus Davidson constructs an ingenious—some would say powerful—argument in behalf of a materialist account of the mind. If Davidson is right, our minds are not immaterial substances. The only way of accounting for the fact that minds cause behavior is by judging that minds are material substances. In a sense, Davidson turns Princess Elizabeth's question into an argument supporting a materialist view of the mind. Unless mental events are describable in physical terms, it is impossible to account for the fact that our minds cause or bring about many of our actions. If mental events are so described—that is, are described in terms of neural or physiological activity of the brain—then our minds are identical with our brains.

3.7   Looking Ahead

Davidson's argument raises a number of interesting questions, some of which concern *causality.* Is it really true that genuine causality requires "lawlike" connections between cause and effect? And what, precisely, *is* a lawlike connection? For the present, I will not address these questions. More will be said concerning the subject of causality in Chapters 8 and 9. My guess is that even if it turns out that Davidson is mistaken in assuming that causality requires lawlike connections, causal arguments of the sort considered in section 3.2 give us good reason to judge that our minds are material things. When we turn our attention away from *people* and consider things such as dogs and cats, very few of us would take seriously the suggestion that the hypothesis of an *immaterial* mind is required to explain canine or feline behavior. Since we naturally and justifiably appeal to psychological facts ("The dog is thirsty") in the course of explaining such behavior ("Why did the dog scratch at the door?"), we naturally assume that animal psychology and animal behavior can be accounted for without resorting to the hypothesis of immaterial animal minds (canine and feline "souls"). Why should the situation be different when we consider people? If Fido can desire water without having an immaterial mind, why can't Alice desire fame, fortune, or gin without having an immaterial mind? If we allow that Fido's mind is Fido's brain, why should we deny that Alice's mind is Alice's brain?

This result hardly encourages the idealist proposal that tables, mountains, and oak trees exist in the mind. If my mind is indeed my brain, then it is rather hard to see how something like a mountain or a tree—something that is considerably larger than any brain— can possibly be located *in* my mind.

However, comparative size may not be the important thing. A thimble is considerably smaller than a normal brain. If we follow Davidson in judging that minds are brains and also say that thimbles exist in minds, then we are committed to saying that thimbles exist in brains. But somehow this does not sound plausible.

Of course Berkeley and his followers argue that on its proper analysis a thimble is no more than a collection of ideas. Surely ideas exist in our minds. If our brains are our minds, then ideas exist, somehow, in our brains. So if thimbles are properly analyzed as collections of ideas, thimbles *do* exist in brains.

But it is hard to take this seriously. As was argued in Chapter 2, there is reason to doubt that things such as thimbles and mountains are really collections of ideas. People who think about Mount Rainier presumably have an *idea* of Mount Rainier in their minds. (So if minds are brains, such people have an idea of this mountain in their brains.) But since the *mountain* itself is not an idea, we cannot conclude from this that the mountain is located in the mind.

Whatever mountains are, we may well doubt that mountains are things that are literally located in our minds.

A mountain is a substantial thing that exists independently of every mind. This sounds plausible but raises new problems. What is a "substantial thing," exactly? Granting that Mount Rainier *is* a substantial thing that exists independently of every mind, precisely what analysis should we give of the nature of this thing? It is to questions such as this that we next turn attention.

There is, of course, much more to be said about the mind. No doubt critics will charge that the proposed identification of something *spiritual* like a mind with something *material* such as a brain is no more plausible than Berkeley's identification of *material* things such as mountains with *spiritual* things such as ideas. I doubt this. But I concede that there is much more to be said about the true nature of the mind. We will return to questions concerning the nature of the mind in Chapter 8.

CHAPTER 4

Substance

. . . a particular is a substance, logically capable of independent existence. It could exist although nothing else existed.

DAVID ARMSTRONG, *NOMINALISM & REALISM* (1978)[1]

To say that an object has objective existence is not to say that it is unknowable or that we cannot have true beliefs about it. It is to say that its existence and nature is in no way dependent on our epistemic capacities. It is not constituted by our knowledge, by the synthesizing power of the mind, nor by our imposition of concepts or theories.

MICHAEL DEVITT, *REALISM & TRUTH* (1984)[2]

4.1 Moore's Commonsense Approach to Metaphysics

The English philosopher G. E. Moore (1873–1958) champions a *commonsense* approach to metaphysical questions. Moore tells us that the most important thing that philosophers try to do is to give a description of "the *whole* of the Universe." Ontological questions pertaining to the *existence* or *being* of things are for Moore equivalent to asking whether something is part of the universe. When we ask whether God, the Loch Ness monster, or photons exist, we are in effect asking whether certain things "belong to the universe"— whether, that is, certain things are really part of the world we inhabit.[3] Whatever common sense has to say about God and photons, it hardly seems to support the idealist hypothesis that everything there is, everything that exists, is either a mind or something that exists in a mind.[4] It is not surprising that Moore rejects idealism.[5]

Does a rejection of *idealism* not commit us to *materialism,* the view that everything there is, everything that is part of the universe, is composed of matter? It is important to see that one can, in theory, reject both idealism and materialism—the view, roughly, that everything real is material. As we saw in the previous chapter, *dualists* do precisely this, arguing that the world contains both material substances such as mountains and immaterial substances such as minds. In our previous discussion of the mind, I indicated some of my own misgivings concerning the claim that minds are immaterial substances. But a rejection of the view that minds are immaterial things does not commit us to materialism. In theory one might—though I do not say one should—both affirm that minds are material substances and deny that everything that is real is material. One might, for example, hold that the number 7 is perfectly real, even though 7 is neither a mind nor a material substance.

Metaphysicians pose the ontological question "What is there?" In doing so, they certainly are not conducting an inventory of each and every thing that exists. Recall a point that was considered in Chapter 1: metaphysics asks questions concerning the general nature of the world we inhabit. Moore certainly would agree with this. He would say that the metaphysician's job is that of taking an inventory not of *each* individual thing but rather of the *kinds* or *sorts* of things there are. We cannot hope to come up with a list of each and every individual that exists in Brooklyn, much less in the entire world (universe). But perhaps we can compile a list of the sorts or kinds of things there are in Brooklyn. Materialists would affirm while idealists and dualists would deny that everything to be found in Brooklyn is material.

How are we to determine what is and is not a genuine *kind* of thing? Our world contains policemen and bankers. Are we here dealing with things of the "same kind"? Are blue-eyed policemen "the same kind of thing" as brown-eyed policemen? Are blue-eyed corrupt policemen the same kind of thing as blue-eyed honest policemen? Is an oak tree the same kind of thing as an ice cream soda? Some people give an affirmative answer to this last question, arguing that ice cream sodas and oak trees are both *material objects*. [6] Others might allow that sodas and trees are both material things yet still deny that sodas and trees are the same kind of thing.

If we follow Moore's commonsense approach to metaphysics, we shall say that the world contains countless material objects. And we shall also say that the world contains *countless acts or states of consciousness*. Moore argued that we know that the world contains both kinds of thing. Indeed, it might be argued that everything that is known to be in the world is such that it is in one of these two categories: every such thing either is a material object or a state of consciousness. If we take this seriously—as Moore for one was prepared to do—we may judge that we need not go into much detail when we describe the world.[7] Describing the world is a matter of offering a kind-inventory of what there is, what really exists. Perhaps such an inventory need have only two entries; perhaps everything there is—everything that exists—is either a material object or an act of consciousness.

Is this metaphysical picture of the world respectable? Though Moore believes that such a picture accords with common sense, he also recognizes that there are potential objections. We can hardly deny, Moore says, that "there certainly are in the Universe *also* at least two other things beside these—things which are neither material objects nor acts of consciousness—namely, Space and Time themselves."[8] An inventory of "what there is" (an ontology) that mentions only material objects and acts of consciousness is thus apparently incomplete. Moore seems to be right when he allows that space and time are *something*. He also seems to be right when he assures us that "it is obvious that they are neither material objects nor acts of consciousness."

On the one hand, Moore allows that space and time are in some sense things. On the other, he argues that space and time are *"unsubstantial* kinds of things."[9] Perhaps the exclusion of space and time from Moore's list of the kinds of things there are is meant to be justified by the proviso that the list is a list of *substantial* kinds of things. There is an obvious problem with this suggestion. This lies with the fact that acts of consciousness somehow do not appear to be substantial kinds of things. (Compare the making of a decision and a coffee cup. Are we here dealing with one substantial thing or two?) Acts of consciousness appear not to deserve a place on Moore's list, assuming that the list is confined to substantial kinds of things. And if the list is not confined to kinds of substantial things, it is not clear why space and time do not deserve a place on the list. Either way there appears to be a problem.

4.2 Aristotle's Primary Substance

Certainly Moore is right about one thing: it is not true that every constituent or part of the world is itself a substantial thing. When we encounter a "substantial thing," we encounter a *substance*. But many of the things we encounter in daily life do not qualify as substances. Consider the following claims:

Alice's smile is enchanting (meaningful, sinister).

John has a nasty habit of smoking in bed.

Alice has a bad cold.

John has a fine voice.

There are many miles between the camp and the summit.

In appropriate contexts, such statements are true. This may encourage the idea that the world contains such "things" as smiles, voices, miles, head colds, and bad habits. We might grant this much and still deny that smiles and miles are substances. Hikers who are faced with "many a mile to go" are not confronted by a series of substantial obstacles standing in the way of their destination. Of course we may deny that miles and smiles are substantial things—substances—without denying that there really are such things as miles and smiles. So doing, we might hold that while it is true that all substances are material, many things that are perfectly real (many things that exist) are not material substances.

How are we to distinguish between substantial kinds of things and unsubstantial kinds of things? Intuitively, the oak tree outside my study window is a substantial thing. Presumably the word "tree" stands for a kind of substantial thing and so stands for a substantial kind of thing. The situation is different when we consider, say, the fragrance of the tree. Though the fragrance of the tree is undeniably a genuine part or constituent of the world, it fails intuitively to qualify as a substantial thing. Since the fragrance is perfectly real, some things that are perfectly real fail to qualify as substances. In accounting for what there is, we must not fail to note that the world contains countless things that are not substantial things (not substances).

The ancient Greek philosopher Aristotle (384–322 B.C.), one of the truly great figures in the history of philosophy, was perhaps the first to call attention to this. Like Moore and many other metaphysicians, Aristotle had a penchant for compartmentalizing things. In Aristotle's *Categories*, we are told that:

A *substance*—that which is called a substance most strictly, primarily, and most of all—is that which is neither said of a subject nor in a subject, e.g., the individual man or the individual horse.[10]

I cannot here come close to doing full justice to the complexity and subtlety of Aristotle's account of the categories of things there are. My concern lies with Aristotle's portrayal of individual men and individual horses (and, by implication, individual trees, ships, hawks, handsaws, etc.) as substantial things in the primary sense—so-called *primary substances.* Is this classification accurate? The passage just cited suggests that Aristotle might have been tempted to say:

> (A1) x is a primary substance (henceforth a substance) if and only if x is neither in a subject nor can be said of a subject.

This rules out a great deal. In some sense, Alice's intelligence (even temper, beauty, headache) is "in" Alice. Assuming that Alice herself qualifies as a "subject," it seems that Alice's intelligence (even temper, etc.) fails to qualify as a substance. But does Alice herself qualify as a substance? Aristotle thinks the question deserves an affirmative answer. But can this assessment of the matter be reconciled with principle (A1)? Suppose that Alice is the mayor of the city in which we live. We then might truly say that the mayor is Alice. Here it may appear that we can say of a certain subject (the mayor) that it (she) is Alice. Since Alice can be "said of" a certain subject, it then might be concluded that Alice fails to satisfy the condition of substancehood that is posed by principle (A1).

Subscribing to the sort of argument just considered, a critic might argue that Aristotle is mistaken in thinking that individual people qualify as substances on his own analysis of substancehood. However, we might doubt that the critic is right about this. One—not the only and perhaps not the best—way of responding to the critic would be to say that Aristotle's analysis of what a substance is should be amended as follows:

> (A2) x is a primary substance (a substance) if and only if x is neither in a subject other than itself nor can be said of a subject other than itself.

There is a good deal more to Alice than her even temper. Since Alice's even temper is in something other than itself (namely, Alice), Alice's even temper fails to meet the condition of substancehood posed by (A2). But since Alice and the mayor are one individual, the mayor is not "a subject other than" Alice herself. So even if Alice can be "said of" the mayor—as in the statement "The mayor is Alice"—this does not show that Alice can be said of a subject other than herself. The critic's argument collapses.

4.3   Qualities

If Alice is a substance, presumably you and I—and people generally—are substances. But what sorts of things qualify as substances? It seems that many words that we frequently apply to things do not name or designate substantial things. Consider the word "red." We may correctly apply this word to the rose in the vase. Redness—a certain color—is in some sense "in" the rose and can be "said of" the rose. But assuming that the rose qualifies as a "subject other than" redness (a color), principle (A2) disqualifies redness from being a substance. Colors are not substances, even though individuals that qualify as substances have color. Lips, roses, berries, and fire trucks are substantial things. The color red—which somehow is *in* lips, roses, berries, and fire trucks—is not itself a substantial thing.

Redness is a *quality* of certain substantial things. The same might be said of laziness, honesty, brittleness, and blueness. In each case we are dealing not with substantial things but with qualities of substantial things. But then what *sort* of thing is a quality? What sort of thing are we dealing with when we consider redness itself? Some people are tempted to say that redness—and qualities generally— are *concepts*. This replaces one question with another: what is a concept?[11]

We might be told that concepts are things that exist only in our minds. Perhaps concepts are *ideas* or at least close relatives of ideas. Presumably nothing that exists only in the mind qualifies as a substantial thing. As followers of Aristotle argue, true substances have "independent existence"—which is to say that they do not logically depend for their existence upon the existence of other things.[12] Alice's smile is not a substance precisely because Alice's smile cannot exist independently of Alice. Perhaps *concepts* are in the same boat. If concepts, like ideas and desires, cannot exist apart from minds, then concepts fail to be substantial things. Thus the suggestion that qualities are concepts appears to support the Aristotelian thesis that qualities are not substantial things. On this view, when we employ the term "red" or speak of redness, we are not speaking of a substantial thing existing outside the mind but rather of a concept existing *in* the mind.

But think about this. The fire truck that occupies the garage across the street presumably is a substantial thing that exists outside our minds. If the term "red" names a concept and concepts exist only in our minds, it is then hard to see how the fire truck can *be* red. How can something *outside* the mind *be* something that is located only *in* the mind?

Somehow it seems that redness, a certain color, really is *in*— really is a feature of—the fire truck. Since the truck exists outside the mind, redness exists outside the mind. The point holds for other qualities: brittleness and blueness and perhaps (though this is controversial) beauty. Qualities are located—qualities exist—*outside* the mind. If concepts exist only *in* the mind, obviously it will not do to identify qualities with concepts.

Of course followers of Berkeley may contest this. For *them*, it is not true that the fire truck exists outside of the mind. One can imagine an argument for the idealist assessment of the situation that runs as follows: (1) redness is a concept existing in the mind, (2) redness is part of (is in) the fire truck, so (3) the fire truck must be in the mind. What about this?

If we follow Aristotle, we will deny that qualities of substantial things are themselves substantial things. However, Aristotle nowhere argues that qualities are *concepts* or that qualities exist merely in the mind. Some theorists *have* suggested something like this. Berkeley seems to be in this camp. Perhaps it was the conviction that qualities exist in minds—conjoined with the belief that things cannot exist apart from their qualities—that led Berkeley to judge that things exist in the mind. Berkeley has allies here. Writing many centuries after Aristotle, Locke argued that general words such as "red" and "blue" are "signs of general ideas."[13] On one interpretation, Locke might be taken to suggest that when we speak of redness or blueness, we are speaking—whether we recognize this or not—of abstract things (ideas, concepts) existing in the mind.

However, this seems to be a mistake. Like lips and roses, the fire truck down the street *is* red. Since the truck does not exist in the mind, redness does not exist in the mind either. If Locke means to suggest that the term "red" names something that exists only in the mind, it is very hard to see how Locke can allow that the truck—

which exists outside the mind—really is red. Things outside the mind *have* qualities. So qualities do not seem to be concepts if concepts are things that exist in the mind.

In short, the present argument in behalf of idealism is questionable. Common sense assures us that red things (roses, fire trucks) are not located in the mind. If common sense is right here, as I think it is, we do well to deny that qualities of things are located in (and not outside) our minds. If concepts are located in minds, then we should deny that redness is a concept. Redness is located in things such as lips, berries, cherries, and fire trucks. Since such things exist outside the mind, redness must exist outside the mind.

4.4   Universals

It is one thing to say what qualities are *not* and quite a different thing to say what qualities *are.* If the color red is not itself a substantial thing and is not a concept, what sort of thing *is* it? What sort of thing is a quality? This is question with a history; it was pursued at length by ancient Greek philosophers such as Aristotle and his teacher Plato (470?–347 B.C.) and is therefore a subject where close study of the history of philosophy is likely to pay dividends. Why did Plato and Aristotle, and many other famous thinkers, theorize at length about qualities? The answer, briefly, is that qualities play a central and indeed indispensable role in comprehending the world in which we live. (Try to describe any portion of the world without mentioning qualities!) It is odd that Moore's inventory of what there is makes no mention of qualities, since a world containing only material objects and acts of consciousness but no qualities is perfectly inconceivable.

Consider the color red. The rose in the vase I see on the mantel is red, as is the fire truck at the corner. The rose and the fire truck are *the same color.* Redness, a certain color, is *in* the fire truck and also *in* the rose. Indeed, redness is in—is a quality of—a great many different substantial things. Jack's tie is red, as is Jill's hat. If the tie presently is in Boston and the hat presently is in New York, it seems that redness, a certain quality, is presently located both in Boston and New York. Thus it appears that one "thing"—a certain quality—is located in two different places at the same time. This is, roughly, what traditional philosophers mean when they argue that qualities are *universals*. To qualify as a universal, a thing does not have to be everywhere. But it must be such that it is, or can be, in different places at one time.

We might judge both that *individual substances* (individual horses, trees, human beings, etc.) are not universals and that *qualities* are universals. If we are correct, this means that no individual can properly be identified with any quality. We can never truly assert that any individual *is* itself a quality. We cannot do this because qualities are universals while individuals are not. No individual can be located in many different places at one time. If Jack's tie is presently in Boston, then it follows that Jack's tie cannot presently be in New York. If the color red is presently in Boston, it does not follow that the color red is not presently in New York. From the fact that injustice can be located in one place, we cannot conclude that injustice is not located in other places as well.

We might judge that every quality is a universal. This does not entail that every universal is a quality. Consider Shakespeare's play *Hamlet*. The play *Hamlet* does not seem to be the same sort of thing as qualities such as redness and wisdom. No person created the color red. But it seems that a certain person did create the play *Hamlet*. Undeniably our world contains *Hamlet*. But where, exactly, is *Hamlet* located? A certain substantial thing presently located on my bookshelf bears the title "Hamlet." Is *this* object Shakespeare's play? I do not think so. We do not destroy Shakespeare's play *Hamlet* when we destroy the book on my shelf. The play continues to exist even when *this* book is destroyed. So the play cannot be *identified* with this book.

Shakespeare's play *Hamlet* is, it seems, presently located in many different places—on many different shelves in many different libraries. If that is so, *Hamlet* qualifies as a universal. However, this does not commit us to the conclusion that *Hamlet* is a quality. It is one thing to say that every quality is a universal and quite another to say that every universal is a quality. We can accept the first claim and still reject the second. Qualities are not created by people, though, of course, people often create substantial things that have qualities. Since Shakespeare created the play *Hamlet*, it appears that this play is not itself a quality of other things. *Hamlet* appears to be a universal but not a quality. *Hamlet* is not a material substance, since no material substance is located in many places at one time.

Nor does *Hamlet* seem to be a concept or idea, since it appears that *Hamlet* exists outside of the mind. We cannot say that everything there is—everything that exists—is either an individual or a quality, since Shakespeare's play appears to be neither.

4.5   The Predication Argument

Many commonplace things are material substances. Such things have certain qualities. But it seems that no material substance *is* itself a quality. For qualities are universals and material substances are not.

Consider a particular rose that grows in a certain garden. This individual, the rose, is a material substance. We may grant this and still wonder what the rose *is*. To what, exactly, do we refer when we speak of the rose? In some ways, the question may sound strange. When we speak of roses—when we employ the expression "this rose"—we refer to *roses*. A rose is a rose is a rose. What else could a rose be?

Unfortunately this does not take us far. The word "rose" is employed to refer to roses. But what sort of thing, exactly, are we speaking of when we speak of roses? We might naturally respond by listing various *qualities* or *attributes* that characterize roses. Thus we might say:

> This rose is red,
> This rose is alive,
> This rose needs water to live,
> . . . .
> This rose smells sweet.

In each case, a certain quality is said to characterize a certain individual—a certain substance. But as Locke and others have argued, there is a potential problem here. Qualities of things fail to be substances themselves. This is illustrated by redness, a certain color. Since redness is "in" things other than itself—for example, in the rose that grows in our garden and the fire truck that stands in the firehouse—redness fails to be a substantial thing. Thus the expression "This rose" that appears to the left of the "is" in the statement

> This rose is red

designates a *substance,* while the expression that appears to the right of the "is"—the word "red"—designates something that is not a substance (a color, quality, or attribute). Obviously we cannot *identify* something that is not a substance (the color red) with something that *is* a substance (our rose). We can, in appropriate circumstances, *identify* the mayor and Alice. Since the mayor *is* Alice, there is nothing more to the mayor than Alice and nothing more to Alice than the mayor. Things do not work this way at all when we say that a rose is red. Though the quality redness is somehow *in* the rose, there is more to the rose than redness. Arguably the point holds true regardless of which quality or attribute we ascribe to any substantial thing. Since no quality is a substance, no quality can be identified with any substance. Predicative statements such as the ones on the list above fail to tell what the expression "this rose" refers to or designates. Such statements direct attention to various qualities. But since qualities are not substances, such statements do not tell us what we are are talking about when we talk about roses. This is the sort of reasoning that leads Locke to observe that:

> . . . if any one will examine himself concerning his notion of
> pure substance in general, he will find that he has no other idea
> of it at all, but only a supposition of he knows not what *support*
> of such qualities. . . .[14]

Our rose has various qualities. But the rose itself, a certain substance, is something distinct from each of these qualities (none of which is itself a substance). We cannot *identify* the rose with any quality. For example, we cannot correctly identify this rose with redness—since we do not destroy the color red when we destroy this rose. We somehow *associate* the substance—the rose—with various qualities that are not themselves substantial things. But the association appears utterly mysterious. Locke seems to believe[15] that the most we can say is that the substance is itself something, *we know not exactly what,* that serves as "a *support* of . . . qualities."[16] Whenever we try to explain what sort of thing a certain substance is, we find ourselves ascribing qualities to this substance. But this does not seem to get us anywhere, since none of these qualities is itself a substance. Substances and qualities seem to be different kinds—if you prefer, different categories—of things entirely. So it is hard to see how we can explain what a substance is by calling attention to any quality.

4.6　Russell's Bundle Theory

If the Lockean argument is sound, substances may appear to be utterly mysterious things. Assuming that we are speaking of substances when we speak of individual things such as people, horses, and fire trucks, it may appear that we are left with the result that we generally do not know what it is we are talking about when we say that the horse is beautiful, the fire truck is red, or the person is unreliable. This is not an encouraging result. But how is it to be avoided? Clearly we need an analysis of substance.

Some theorists argue that substantial things such as roses are in fact nothing more than collections or "bundles" of qualities. If a basketball or baseball team is nothing more than a collection of people, then why cannot an individual substance be analyzed as nothing more than a collection of certain *qualities*—namely, all and only the qualities this substance "has"?

At one time, the English philosopher Bertrand Russell (1872–1970) defended this position.[17] To understand what Russell is saying, perhaps it will help to turn our attention away from roses for the moment. Consider, if you will, a basketball team (the Celtics, say) that has ten members. We may say that Smith (a certain player) is on this team, that Jones is on the team, and so on. But what, exactly, is this thing that Smith and Jones are "on"? The Celtics' team hardly can be *identified* with Smith, or with Jones, or . . . with any individual player. The team certainly is "something more" than any particular player. Must we then conclude that the team is some mysterious thing (something we know not what) that individual players are on? It seems not. One thing we might say is that the Celtics' team is in fact a certain collection—bundle, if you will—of individual players. Even though it is true that the Celtics' team cannot be identified with any particular player, it is false that the Celtics' team is a mysterious entity. There is a middle position that lies between identifying the team with some individual player and judging that the team is a mysterious and unknowable entity. This position is that the Celtics' team is a collection (bundle) of certain individuals—the individuals "on" the team, as we normally say.

Russell's *bundle analysis* of roses bears a certain similarity to this middle position with respect to teams. It is true that a rose cannot be identified with the color red or with any single quality. But it does not follow that Locke and his disciples are right in judging that a rose is a "something we know not what" that supports various qualities. Russell proposes that we steer a course between two implausible positions by saying that a rose is a collection, a bundle, of various qualities. We might normally say that a rose "has" a certain quality, much as we might normally say that Smith is "on" the Celtics' team. But the "has" and "on" locutions may be misleading, suggesting, as they do, that roses and teams are something apart from qualities and players respectively. Much as we might judge that the team is really a collection of people, defenders of the bundle analysis, such as Russell, argue that ordinary things such as roses are in reality collections of various qualities.[18] Just as it is a mistake to suppose that there is more to a team than the various players on it, it is also a mistake to judge that there is more to a substantial thing than the various qualities that are predicated of the thing in question. In short, things such as roses are collections of qualities. This does not mean that a rose is a collection of ideas, as Berkeley thought, or a collection of mind-dependent concepts. For the qualities of things exist outside and are independent of our minds. Since bundle theorists are not committed to idealism, arguments opposing idealism carry no weight in opposition to the bundle theory.

Teams appear to be one sort of thing while (individual) players are another. Clearly things of the former sort (teams) cannot exist unless things of the latter sort do. How could it happen that the world contains, say, a football team but no football players?

The situation is similar when we turn to substantial things and their qualities. Clearly things (substances) cannot exist unless qualities do. How could there be a thing that *has* no qualities—a "naked" substance, so to speak? Clearly substances lacking qualities cannot exist. And it might be proposed that whenever the existence of x's requires the existence of y's, it must be true that y's are constituents of x's. If that is so, qualities appear to be constituents of substances. And it is a short step from this to the conclusion that a substantial thing is nothing more than a collection or bundle of qualities.

But if qualities are really *universals* and substantial things are not, it then seems that the constituents of substantial things (qualities, namely) are completely different sorts of things than are substances themselves. Is this possible? Can x's really be made up or composed of y's if y's and x's are completely different sorts of things?

I think this is possible. Intuitively, the individual players on a basketball team are different sorts of things than the team they are on. For one thing, the individuals on the team have arms and legs, brothers and sisters, and hopes and fears. No *team* is in this position. Considered individually, the constituents of a thing are often quite different from the thing of which they are parts. So the bundle theory cannot be dismissed on the grounds that it commits us to judging that things of one sort (substances) are composed of radically different sorts of things (qualities). This judgment is perfectly true.

4.7   An Argument Opposing the Bundle Theory

In theory, it seems that for each individual substance there is a list of all and only the qualities that are, as we would normally say, possessed by this individual. If Russell is right, it seems that each individual can correctly be identified with the sum or totality of qualities that appears on such a list. But *is* Russell right? I doubt it. Consider any substance you like, say the tree outside my window. Can this tree be identified with some collection or bundle of qualities? If so, with which collection exactly? The question proves surprisingly difficult to answer. Let {Fall Tree} be the collection (set) of all and only the qualities that my tree "has" in the fall and {Spring Tree} be the collection (set) of all and only the qualities that my tree "has" the following spring. Since the tree in question is yellow in the fall and green in the spring, this means that the quality of yellowness is and the quality of greenness is not a member of {Fall Tree}, while the quality of greenness is and the quality of yellowness is not a member of {Spring Tree}. Since {Fall Tree} and {Spring Tree} have different quality members, {Fall Tree} and {Spring Tree} clearly are different collections of qualities (or different sets). But how does the *tree* outside my window fit into the picture? If we say that the tree is {Fall Tree}, then we must deny that the tree is {Spring Tree}. (We cannot identify *one* thing with two *different* things!) But {Spring Tree} appears to have no less claim to being the tree in question than does {Fall Tree}.

Bundle theorists may not be much impressed by this objection. They may reply that the objection fails to take seriously the plain fact that things *change* over periods of time. As we shall soon see, the topic of change raises a number of fundamental metaphysical questions. Since it is best to address these questions directly, I shall say no more about the first objection to the bundle theory.

Let us pursue instead a second line of objection to the bundle theory. It is certainly plausible to judge that for each presently existing individual in the world there is a unique list of qualities—a list such that only *this* individual presently "has" all and only the qualities on this list. Can one such list then correspond to two or more individuals? Perhaps this does not in fact happen. Nonetheless, it seems to be in theory *possible* for two individuals to have all and only the same qualities. A wealthy Texan might have architects build an exact replica of the Eiffel Tower in downtown Dallas. Qualitatively speaking, the replica—we might call it "the Leffie Tower"—might appear to be *exactly* like the original (the Eiffel Tower itself—the real thing). If things really are as they appear, the Leffie Tower and the Eiffel Tower are then *two* individuals that have all and only the same qualities. One list of qualities corresponds to two distinct substances.

In actuality it is unlikely that this sort of situation ever arises. We might grant this and still judge that such a situation is theoretically possible. If it *is* possible, bundle theorists have a problem—namely, that it is not possible for two things to be correctly identified with one thing.

Bundle theorists assure us that substantial things such as buildings can correctly be identified with collections of qualities or attributes. But if two substances can have all and only the same qualities, then bundle theorists would apparently have to say that it is possible for two substantial things to be such that each can correctly be identified with one collection of qualities (the collection whose quality members are "had" by each of the two things in question). Since it is not even possible for two things to be correctly identified with one thing, the bundle theory must be rejected.

The second objection to the bundle theory is itself open to certain objections. Surely any two things we consider will always be located in different places. Since things located in different places stand in different spatial relations to other things, the fact of differing location seems to guarantee different (relational) qualities. Since the Leffie Tower is located in Dallas and the Eiffel Tower in Paris, the Leffie Tower is much closer to Houston than is the Eiffel

Tower. Even if it is possible for the two towers to be precisely alike—*indiscernible,* as philosophers say—with respect to their "pure" nonrelational qualities, these towers still are quite different (discernible) when we consider their "impure" relational qualities. The Leffie Tower has but the Eiffel Tower lacks the relational quality of being close to some of the world's largest cattle ranches and oilfields. It appears, more generally, that two individuals cannot possibly have the same relational qualities, since two things cannot be in one place at the same time. Since things that are located in different places must have different relational qualities, it seems that two things cannot be indiscernible. But the second objection to the bundle theory rests on the assumption that two things *can* be indiscernible. So the second objection fails.

Or does it? Imagine a world containing two spheres (A and B, say) and nothing else. Conceivably sphere A and sphere B might be indistinguishable with respect to "pure" qualities. If sphere A is black, sphere B is black; if A weighs 100 pounds, then B weighs 100 pounds, and so on. Is there then any intrinsic qualitative respect in which A and B differ? It is hard to see how the question can be answered affirmatively. Indeed, it seems theoretically possible that A and B have precisely the same relational properties. For example, both A and B might have the relational quality of being a certain distance away from a black sphere weighing 100 pounds. It seems possible that *two* spheres could be in all intrinsic and relational respects exactly the same.[19] Note that the claim is not that there really *are* such "indiscernible" spheres. The claim is rather that it is possible that there *could* be two such spheres. The mere *possibility* of such a thing happening poses a threat to the bundle theory of particulars. If the bundle theory were correct, then it seems that it would be impossible for two things to be qualitatively indistinguishable in all respects. Since this is not theoretically impossible, we can conclude that the bundle theory is not correct.

4.8   An Alternative to the Bundle Theory

You may not be convinced that it really is possible for two things to be in all respects indiscernible; therefore you may be less than impressed by the second objection to the bundle theory. Even so, you should anticipate further difficulties for bundle analyses of commonplace things. One problem arises from the fact that the relation of parthood is transitive: if x has y as a constituent or part and y, in turn, has z as a constituent or part, then it must be the case that x has z as a constituent or part. This plain fact poses problems for bundle theorists.

Suppose the bundle theory were right. Then when we say that Jill's hat is red, we are in effect saying that redness, a certain universal, is part of Jill's hat. Since parthood is transitive, anything that is part of redness must then be part of Jill's hat.

It is true that the color red is located in Wyoming. (Of course red is located in many other places as well, but let us stick with Wyoming for the moment.) Here we seem to be saying that one thing—the color red—itself has a certain feature or quality, namely, the quality of being located in Wyoming. But how should we interpret "has"? Bundle theorists assure us that when we say of Jill's hat that it *has* the quality of being red, we are really saying that the quality red is *part* of Jill's hat. If things work this way in the hat case, then presumably things also work this way when we say that the color red itself has the quality of being located in Wyoming. Interpreting "has" in terms of parthood, this last claim appears to be equivalent to saying that the quality of being located in Wyoming is part of the color red.

We seem to be left with the result that both statements (1) and (2), as follows, are true:

(1) Red (a quality) is part of Jill's hat.

(2) Being located in Wyoming (another quality) is part of red.

Since the parthood relation is transitive, it follows that

(3) Being located in Wyoming (a quality) is part of Jill's hat.

This is equivalent to saying that

(4) Jill's hat is (has as a constituent the quality of being) located in Wyoming.

The problem is that (4) is false. As it happens, Jill's hat is located in Boston and not in Wyoming. Jill's hat *never* was or will be (we may suppose) located in Wyoming. So something has gone wrong. The case illustrates that a quality of a quality of a hat may fail to be a quality of the hat itself. And this suggests that it is a mistake to interpret the *having* of qualities in terms of parthood or constituency. It is true that Jill's hat *has* the quality of being red. But there is reason to think that it is false that the quality of redness is a *part* of Jill's hat.

I believe that this argument, and other arguments that I cannot review here, casts grave doubt upon the proposal that substantial things such as hats are properly identified with collections of qualities. Common sense accepts this verdict. Suppose that we are told that a *smile* or a *frown* is located in a certain room. Surely if a smile is indeed located in the room, there must be a *smiler*—an individual who smiles—in this room. The point carries over from smiles and frowns (things people do) to *qualities* generally. Unhappiness cannot be in a room unless this room contains a *subject* who is unhappy. Redness likewise requires a subject. If redness is in a certain place, surely there must be some subject, some individual, that is red in this place. Qualities do not float around on their own. Common sense assures us that qualities are in some sense *attached* to certain things.[20]

If correct, this suggests that bundle theorists are very much on the wrong track. Qualities require a subject, so the subject—the individual substance that smiles, is unhappy, or is red—can hardly be reduced to (a bundle of) qualities. This sounds right. But it leaves us with a problem. It seems that we are not speaking of any quality or any bundle of qualities when we speak of an individual substance such as the oak tree outside my window. But then what *are* we speaking of when we refer to this tree? What *is* a tree, anyway, if not a bundle of qualities?

In the next chapter we will turn to a quite different—and I suspect somewhat more promising—approach to the matter. There is, of course, more to be said concerning Russell's bundle theory. But I think enough has been said to suggest that Russell and his followers are barking up the wrong tree. Although we correctly predict or ascribe various qualities to any substance we encounter, no substance can correctly be identified with the sum of its qualities.

There is more—much more—to be said about qualities themselves. Some theorists would argue, contrary to what was suggested earlier (section 4.4), that qualities are not properly viewed as *universals*. I cannot review the arguments for this position here. I can only record my conviction that whatever the proper analysis of qualities may be, it cannot be true (contrary to Berkeley) that qualities are ideas, or things that exist merely in our minds. Substantial things simply cannot exist without qualities. Since substantial things exist outside our minds, qualities cannot exist merely in our minds.

CHAPTER 5

Parts and Wholes

Traditionally metaphysics aspires to trace what there is, meaning what the ultimate reality is on which everything depends.

JOHN F. POST, *THE FACES OF EXISTENCE* (1987)[1]

Thus, we have reached the result that some things are different from the sum of their parts; we may call such things wholes.

ROBERT NOZICK, *PHILOSOPHICAL EXPLANATIONS* (1981)[2]

. . . it is evident that I cannot distinguish innumerable parts in any particular line, surface, or solid . . . whereof I conclude they are not contained in it.

GEORGE BERKELEY, *A TREATISE CONCERNING THE PRINCIPLES OF HUMAN KNOWLEDGE* (1710)[3]

5.1 Are Commonplace Things Collections of Molecules?

Substances are often said to be, in theory, independent of other things. If we grant that the oak tree outside my window is a substance, then—since ideas do not appear to exist independently of minds or thinking beings—we must presumably reject the idealist proposal that this tree is an idea or a collection of ideas. What analysis can then be given of the tree? In Chapter 4, we saw that there is reason to doubt that commonplace things such as oak trees can correctly be analyzed as collections of *qualities*. But perhaps we can reject both the view that a tree is a collection of *ideas* and the view that a tree is a collection of *qualities*. So doing, we might say that the tree located outside my window is nothing more than a certain collection of microscopic entities (cellulose molecules). Expanding on this, we might judge that macroscopic material things generally are properly identifiable with collections of microscopic entities. This sounds like an account that is scientifically respectable. If we accept this account, we may well reject a suggestion made by Sir Arthur Eddington:

> There are duplicates of every object about me—two tables, two chairs, two pens. . . . One of them has been familiar to me from earliest childhood. It is a commonplace object of that environment I call the world. . . . [A]bove all, [a commonplace thing] is *substantial.* . . . My scientific table is mostly emptiness. Sparsely scattered in that emptiness are numerous electrical charges rushing about with great speed.[4]

If Eddington is right, I am presently sitting on not one but *two* chairs and writing upon not one but *two* tables. This proposal is very strange indeed. Why not say that the commonplace table at which I am sitting *is* the scientific table at which I am sitting? (If the scientific table is, in the last analysis, made up of electrical charges, then the commonplace table is made up of electrical charges.) Why not?

One potential problem lies with the fact that it is not clear that the analysis of commonplace tables and trees as collections of microscopic entities can be reconciled with the plausible thesis that things such as tables and trees qualify as genuine substances. To explain why that is so, some stage setting is required.

5.2   The Quest for Substance

There are those who would argue that when you scratch a metaphysician you will find a frustrated theoretical physicist. Anyone can form respectable beliefs about garden-variety macroscopic things such as tables, trees, and dogs. But we may suspect that a deeper understanding of the world in which we live forces us to recognize the fact that the really fundamental building blocks of the world are entities that cannot be *seen, touched,* or *tasted.* Perhaps substances—"substantial things" in the truest sense—are in this category. There was a time when many theorists thought that "atoms" were the really basic entities that inhabit our world. Today we know that this view is radically misconceived. In a wonderful essay expressing the joy, excitement, and frustration of doing work in contemporary physics, Jeremy Bernstein observes that modern physics is concerned with "a completely unexpected world of elementary particles":

> A few new particles might not have been so difficult to digest. But they kept appearing, on what seemed a weekly basis. Enrico Fermi remarked that elementary-particle physics was getting to be like botany, and Oppenheimer proposed that a prize be given to an experimenter who did *not* find a new particle.[5]

Must the discovery of new particles ever come to an end? Will we ever arrive at a point where science has discovered all that there is to discover in the microscopic realm? I'll return to this in a moment. First a word concerning the relation between macroscopic things such as oak trees and microscopic things such as molecules. In theory, it seems possible for things such as molecules to exist even though things such as oak trees do not. But this does not work the other way round: it is *not* possible for trees to exist without molecules. And of course this point does not hold merely for trees. It seems to be *generally* true that macroscopic material things depend for their existence upon the existence of microscopic things such as molecules. In short, it appears that tables, trees, cats, and dogs are not independent of molecules and so do not qualify as substances on the independence analysis of substances.

Are molecules then true substances? It seems not, since there are other "more fundamental" entities of which molecules are composed. What about atoms? As it turned out, atoms are not "atomic" in the sense of not being composed of still more fundamental entities. As Bernstein's comments suggest, to this day science has failed to discover entities that have clear claim to being regarded as really *elementary*, rock-bottom constituents of our world. In this sense, scientists have failed to discover the substance of the world.

But is "substance" there to be discovered? Trees can be explained in terms of molecules, molecules in terms of atoms, atoms in terms of electrons and protons. *Must* there be an end to this process of explaining one sort of thing in terms of other sorts of things? Some people are convinced that the question deserves a positive answer. Such people insist that the process of explaining one thing in terms of other, more fundamental things cannot fail to come to an end. But are these people right?

Suppose that we were to accept the following assumptions:

(1) *x* is a substance only if *x* is independent of other things.
(2) Every compound entity is such that it depends upon the existence of more fundamental entities for its existence.
(3) More fundamental entities do not depend for their existence upon the existence of less fundamental entities.

Each of these principles may look plausible enough. Descartes defended (1), saying: "By substance, we can understand nothing else than a thing which so exists that it needs no other thing in order to exist."[6] What are the implications of this? Assuming that (2) is correct, it then appears that no "compound" thing qualifies as a genuine substance. Since every tree and table is a compound thing, it follows that no tree or table is a substance. Indeed, it it hard to see how *any* material object can qualify as a substance. Every material object is such that it is spatially extended—that is, such that it has a certain size and shape. Anything that is extended in space must be such that in theory it can be divided into parts. In short, every material object appears to be a compound thing and thus dependent upon the more elementary things that are its components. On this view, no material thing is a substance. This does not imply that everything that exists is "spiritual" in some sense. As the case of smiles and frowns suggests, a great many things exist that are not substances. Even if no substance is a material thing, it does not follow that everything there is is immaterial.

5.3   Monads

But can it plausibly be said that no material thing is a substance? At least one prominent figure in the history of philosophy, Gottfried Leibniz (1646–1716), seems to have seen things this way.

> . . . we have no need to say that matter is nothing, but it suffices to say that it is a phenomenon like the rainbow; and that it is not a substance, but a result of substances. . . .[7]

Leibniz's views are very subtle and his texts are subject to different interpretations. Nonetheless, it is clear that Leibniz believed in the reality of simple, or indivisible, things which he called "monads." He apparently believed, also, that commonplace material things are somehow to be analyzed as aggregates or collections of monads. It is not entirely clear why Leibniz thought that "there must be monads if things exist at all."[8] Perhaps the reasoning runs as follows: The idea that everything there is, everything that exists, is a collection of other more fundamental things is absurd. Since this idea is absurd (since the idea could not possibly be right), somewhere along the line there must be entities that in theory cannot be analyzed in terms of their components or parts. Such entities—*monads,* as Leibniz calls them—have no parts and so are indivisible. Obviously commonplace things such as oak trees do not qualify as monads. Leibniz suggests in some passages that commonplace material things are not "absolutely real."[9] In other places he seems to allow that material things have a sort of derivative reality, observing that "matter or extended mass in itself can never be more than a *plura entia"* (a plurality of things).[10] The tree outside my window is at best a plurality of substances (monads) and not itself a substance. Just as a collection of marbles is not itself a marble, Leibniz apparently would deny that a collection of genuine substances is itself a genuine substance.

What are monads like? One point is clear: a thing that has no components or parts cannot be analyzed in terms of its components or parts. Perhaps we can explain what a tree is like by talking about cellulose molecules. And perhaps molecules can be analyzed in terms of atoms. But we cannot proceed in the same way when it comes to perfectly simple things that have no components or parts. We cannot analyze monads in terms of their constituents, since monads do not *have* constituents.

There is reason to believe that Leibniz viewed monads as individuals having some sort of (perhaps primitive) "perception" and thus as psychological beings. If monads are not material things, then perhaps monads are in some sense *minds* or at any rate mindlike entities.[11] On first hearing, this proposal may sound utterly implausible. But consider someone who reasons as follows:

> Material things are not simple or indivisible and so do not qualify as monads. Since monads are not material things, monads do not have sizes or shapes. Monads are *immaterial* things that lack the qualities or characteristics we ascribe to material things such as trees and tables. But then what *can* monads be like? The only conceivable answer seems to be that monads are some sort of spiritual entities—*souls* or *minds* that have, perhaps at some very primitive level, a faculty of perception.

I suspect that Leibniz might have been in sympathy with such reasoning, though he seems to reject the suggestion that monads are capable of the full range of psychological functions that characterize a normal person. (We are assured that monads "do not know that they are, or what they are," and that they have no "moral qualities."[12]) Perhaps it is not too far from the mark to say that for Leibniz monads are immaterial and indivisible things having the status of very *primitive* minds.

5.4   A Compositional Regression

Some of us are skeptical of the suggestion that commonplace things such as oak trees are aggregates of minds. This sounds, if not downright crazy, like a claim that may be difficult to justify. Perhaps the oak tree outside my window can be analyzed in terms of cellulose molecules which, in turn, can be analyzed in terms of still more elementary microscopic entities. We may doubt that somewhere down the line—at some point in the process of analyzing one sort of thing in terms of still more fundamental sorts of things—we will arrive at *minds* (or psychological individuals of any sort).

But if this is our position, we are left with some very tough questions. Cells, molecules, electrons, and protons do not appear to qualify as substances in the sense specified by principle (1) above. (1) and (2) together suggest that we move from the less substantial to the more substantial as we proceed to analyze compound things in terms of their constituents. But if this process of analysis does not end with minds, where *does* it end? For reasons mentioned already, the process certainly does not seem to end with any material thing. And if material things do not fill the bill, what is left besides "minds"? If everything that exists is in either the "mind" or "matter" category and if matter fails to qualify as substance, it seems that we must conclude that Leibniz was right: the only genuine substances are minds of some sort.

This might sound persuasive. However, we should note that there is a hidden assumption behind the line of reasoning just considered—namely, that the process of analyzing one thing in terms of other, more fundamental things must come to an end.

Is that so? It certainly appears that if this process does *not* come to an end, there are no genuine substances in the sense of (1). But why cannot things work out this way? Why cannot everything be such that it is in theory analyzable in terms of still more elementary things?[13]

Many people assume that it is simply impossible for a series of successively dependent things to "go on forever" or to fail to terminate. It is by no means clear that this assumption is true. Why must the task of analyzing one sort of thing in terms of more elementary—and some would say more substantial—things ever come to an end?

It may be objected that such a process would leave us with an impossible "infinite regress." But further argument is required before it is clear that the present regress is either infinite or impossible. In a paper entitled "Infinite Regress Arguments," the American philosopher David H. Sanford points out that a "looping" series with neither a first nor last member may fail to be infinite.[14] For example, we encounter a series that *loops* when we consider a situation in which John loves Mary, Mary loves Peter, Peter love Marsha, and Marsha loves John. Even though this series does not come to an end, it fails to be "infinite" in the sense of connecting an infinite number of individuals. From the fact that the process of analyzing one sort of thing in terms of other sorts of things has no end, it does not follow that this process must relate an infinite number of different sorts of things. That much is shown by looping series of the sort illustrated by the case of the lovers above.

But, on reflection, it is hard to see how the process of *decomposition*—the process of analyzing one sort of thing in terms of more elementary things—can fail to be infinite if it does not end. If oak trees are analyzed in terms of cellulose molecules and cellulose molecules are, in turn, analyzed in terms of atoms, it is very hard to see how atoms can then be analyzed in terms of oak trees. In short, it is hard to see how the series corresponding to the relation "*x*'s are composed of *y*'s" can *loop*. And if this series cannot loop, it is infinite if it really goes on without end.

We might grant all of this and still wonder whether there *can* be an endless series of compositional relations in which more complex things are made up of less complex things. Why should it not be possible that, for each level of analysis in which one kind of thing is analyzed in terms of still other sorts of things, there is a further step of compositional analysis that proceeds the same way? We might reject both the view that the ultimate building blocks of the world are "minds," as Leibniz proposed, and the view that they are material things. In so doing, we might deny that there are any such *ultimate* building blocks.

Some people are reluctant to accept this view. Their resistance can perhaps be traced to the conviction that the world must be inhabited by substantial things. In light of assumptions (1) and (2), it seems that there are substantial things, substances, only if there are *simple* things lacking constituents—objects which fill the role of ultimate building blocks. To deny that the process of analyzing things in terms of their components comes to an end is thus to deny, implausibly, that the world contains substances.

Is there a way out? I think we do well not to equate the concept of substance with the concept of things that are independent of other things. Conceivably it is true both that the oak tree outside my window is a substance and that trees depend for their existence upon the existence of cellulose molecules. This suggests that (1) may turn out to be false. Perhaps philosophers like Aristotle and Descartes are mistaken in suggesting that substantial things must be entirely independent of other things. Those of us who believe that this is so are left with a question: What analysis of substance is to be substituted in place of the independence criterion?

5.5 Dependent Substances

We might reject the independence criterion of substancehood and instead maintain that substances are *things that have qualities.* Since the oak tree outside my window has qualities—the tree is *alive* and it is *deciduous*—it thus qualifies as a substance. Since the tree cannot in theory exist unless certain other things (namely, cellulose molecules) exist, we seem to have located a substantial thing that fails the independence test.

Should we accept this? On the present analysis, anything that has qualities is a substance. This has the plausible corollary that commonplace things such as dogs, cats, and trees are substances. Nonetheless there is a problem. Most of us resist the suggestion that words such as "red" and "lazy" designate substantial things. The term "red" names a certain color, a *quality,* and not a substantial thing. The problem lies with the fact that qualities themselves appear to have qualities. For example, the color red has the quality of being the color of Jack's new car. If we say that anything that has qualities is a substantial thing, we must conclude that the color red is itself a substantial thing. This does *not* sound right. Unlike Jack's car, the color red does not seem to qualify as a substantial thing. Note that we can grant that the color red is real—that there *is* such a thing as the color red—without thereby being committed to saying that the color red is a substance. Alice's smile is perfectly real even though it is not a substance.

Perhaps we can do better. We might say that *x* is a substance if and only if it is true both that *x* has qualities and that *x* is not a *universal*—that is, not something that can be multiply located in many places at the same time. Assuming that qualities are universals, this analysis of substance rules out redness as a substance. Since the term "red" names a universal—something that is located in many different places at one time—it does not name a substantial thing. It is a fact that Jack's car is red. Jack's car is a substantial thing, though redness—the color of the car—is not. Both Jack's car and redness are things that have qualities. What disqualifies redness as a substance is the fact that redness is, unlike Jack's car, a universal.

Our present analysis of substance is not without virtues. On the one hand, it enables us to say, plausibly, that commonplace things such as dogs, cats, and automobiles are substances. On the other hand, it implies—again plausibly—that qualities of things are not themselves substantial things.

However, further questions arise. Precisely *what* is it that is named or designated by expressions such as "Jack's car" and "the tree outside my window"? As we saw in the last chapter, there is reason to question the idea that we are speaking of collections or bundles of *qualities* when we refer to automobiles and trees. But if the tree outside my window is not a collection of qualities, precisely what is it? What exactly can the tree *be* if it cannot properly be identified with the sum or totality of its various qualities?

Most of us find it hard to sympathize with Locke's defeatist suggestion that we are speaking of a "something we know not what" when we speak of a substantial thing such as a tree. Are we forced to choose between the Lockean view of substances as mysterious things that somehow *support* qualities and the quite different (Russellian) view that a substance is a sum or bundle of qualities? The contemporary Australian philosopher David Armstrong takes this to be *the* "great question" the resolution of which is required before we will arrive at a respectable theory of substance.[15] On reflection, we might judge that Armstrong's question clearly deserves a negative answer. We can reject both Russell's view that the tree outside the window is a bundle of qualities and Locke's proposal that the tree is a mysterious something that supports various qualities. Let us consider one such approach to substance.

5.6   A Summational Analysis

We might argue that commonplace substances such as trees, cars, and dogs are nothing more than the sum of their various parts. Since a thing's *qualities* are not properly regarded as genuine *parts* of it (as we saw in section 4.7), the various qualities or attributes of the tree outside my window are not *parts* of the tree. For example, the term "deciduous" names a *quality* of the tree but not a *part* of the tree.[16] If the quality of being deciduous—a quality my tree has and my fountain pen lacks—were part of my tree, then the quality of being deciduous would itself be a substance. But this quality is not a substance since it is a universal—and since universals fail to qualify as substantial things. Therefore this quality is not part of my tree.

More generally, it appears that qualities are not *parts* of commonplace substances. But this leaves us with a problem. We are told that my tree is nothing more than the sum of its parts. Since the tree's various qualities are not parts of the tree, the tree is not the sum of its qualities. What, then, is it the sum of? What sorts of things qualify as parts of the tree?

Here perhaps physics offers a way of dealing with a metaphysical question. Physics tells us that a certain collection of microscopic entities—a certain collection of cellulose molecules—is located outside my window. Perhaps each of the microscopic substances qualifies as part of the tree outside my window. To put it another way, perhaps the *tree* is nothing more than the totality or sum of all of the cellulose molecules that make up this collection of molecules. This certainly *sounds* plausible. For one thing, the tree outside my window *coexists with*—is located in precisely the same place as—the collection of cellulose molecules in question. Presumably *two* things do not exist in the same place at the same time. If not, we certainly have reason to conclude that my tree can correctly be identified with the sum of its molecular parts.

Moreover, unlike qualities of the tree, no molecular part of the tree is a universal. (No particular molecule is located in many different places at one time.) Since cellulose molecules themselves have qualities and also fail to be universals, cellulose molecules are themselves substantial things. Such substances are microscopic parts of the macroscopic substance that is the tree outside my window. More generally, every macroscopic substance—every dog, cat, table, and tree—is itself a totality or sum of substantial microscopic entities. Eddington was wrong in suggesting that I am presently sitting at not one but two tables. Eddington's so-called scientific table (namely, a certain collection of microscopic entities) just *is* his so-called commonplace table. The problem of substance is thus resolved.

5.7   Laurel and Hardy

Or is it? Certainly Aristotle and his followers will deny that the present account of substance is correct. As one contemporary Aristotelian says, "a substance is not simply whatever happens to be occupying a particular place at a particular time; for matter fits that description, and matter is not substance."[17] Aristotelians do not deny that the various cellulose molecules that are located in a certain spatial region outside my window are genuine parts of my tree. They *do* deny that the tree itself is nothing more than the sum of its molecular parts. A whole (substance) cannot be identified with the sum of its parts.

To see what Aristotelians are getting at, perhaps it will help us to focus on Laurel and Hardy, the famous comedy team. We might judge that the Laurel-and-Hardy team is nothing more than the totality or sum of its parts—namely, the person who is Laurel and the person who is Hardy. This sounds plausible. What more can there be to a two-person comedy team than the totality of the two individuals (the two people) who make up this team?

But consider the following situation. Before the team of Laurel and Hardy is formed, it happens (we imagine) that an audition is held for a comedy role in a certain film. Laurel shows up for the audition, as does Hardy. The two men have never met until the moment when they nod hello and sit side by side waiting for their respective auditions. At this time the *pair* Laurel and Hardy is located in a certain waiting room. What does *not* yet exist is the comedy *team* of Laurel and Hardy. The comedy team comes into existence only some time later, after Laurel and Hardy have become acquainted and have decided that their merged talents might pay dividends. It thus appears that there is *more to* the team than the pair of individuals who make it up. This pair of individuals—Laurel, on one hand, and Hardy, on the other—existed before the comedy team did. So obviously the team cannot correctly be identified with the pair—the totality of individuals who are part of the team.

The same sort of point might be made in a different way. For suppose that the team of Laurel and Hardy breaks up in, say, 1940. Suppose, too, that, by chance, Laurel and Hardy share adjoining seats on a certain bus in 1950. If the Laurel-and-Hardy comedy team were nothing more than the sum of its parts, the team would still exist in 1950—since the *pair* still exists in 1950. But the Laurel-and-Hardy team does *not* still exist in 1950. So we must reject the suggestion that the team is nothing more than the sum of its individual parts.

The same sort of argument might be offered against the suggestion that the tree outside my window is the sum or totality of its molecular constituents. Suppose that $\{M1, M2, M3, \ldots Mn\}$ is the totality of the molecules that presently are parts of my tree. Can my tree be identified with the sum of these microscopic individuals? Followers of Aristotle will argue that the answer is no. My tree has existed outside my window for many years. Ten years ago this tree was struck by lightning. Can the same thing be said for the totality of molecules $\{M1, M2, M3, \ldots Mn\}$? It seems not, since *this* totality of molecules did not exist ten years ago. (Individual molecules come and go during the period my tree exists. Trees do not always have the same molecular constituents or parts.) Thus certain things that are true of my tree are not true of the sum of its present molecular constituents. Therefore my tree cannot correctly be *identified* with the totality $\{M1, M2, M3, \ldots Mn\}$.

A similar argument can be formulated in opposition to the suggestion that any macroscopic substance can be identified with the totality of its parts. Suppose that Jack, in a used car, undertakes a cross-country trip from California to New York. Sadly, the adventure is marked by repeated automotive breakdowns. Various parts of Jack's car have to be replaced along the way. Indeed, the replacement process, although piecemeal, is so extensive that the car that eventually arrives in New York is made up of entirely different parts than was the car that earlier left California. Nonetheless, followers of Aristotle judge that the arrival car *is* the departure car. Much as one tree may have different molecular constituents at different times—and in time may be composed of entirely different molecules than it was originally—one car can have different carburetors, different tires, different fenders (and so on) at different times.

Aristotle did not use these examples. (He lived more than two thousand years before automobiles or the team of Laurel and Hardy existed.) Nonetheless I think these examples may help to illustrate what Aristotle was driving at when he wrote:

> It seems most distinctive of substance that what is numerically one and the same is able to receive contraries.[18]

Substances undergo *changes* in a way that mere sums of microscopic entities do not. The Redskins' (football) team may thus be a *winner* one year and a *loser* the next—"receiving" contrary qualities at different times—and so may change in a way that no totality of individual people (players, coaches) changes. Similarly, my oak tree may be beleafed—covered with leaves—one month and without leaves the next. This tree may undergo genuine *changes* that no sum of cellulose molecules undergoes. From this fact, as they take it to be, Aristotelians conclude that the tree cannot be identified with any sum of molecules. It is true that the molecules that make up the totality {M1, M2, M3, . . . Mn} are at present genuine parts of the tree outside my window. But it is false that the tree is the same thing as this totality of molecules. Trees, automobiles, and other macroscopic entities cannot be identified with the sum or aggregate of their components.

5.8   Armstrong's Great Question Revisited

The suggestion that substantial things such as trees might be properly identified with the sum of their microscopic parts offered promise of an affirmative answer to Armstrong's great question: Can we reject the view that things such as trees are bundles of qualities without being forced to agree that a tree is a mysterious "something we know not what"? But if the Aristotelian arguments we have reviewed are sound, it was a false promise. Unhappily, we appear to be back where we started, without an acceptable account of the substantial things that populate the world. How should we proceed?

We might begin by identifying and carefully examining the assumptions that underlie the Aristotelian rejection of the view, which many people find plausible, that a substantial thing is nothing more than the sum of its various parts. Perhaps the Aristotelian argument for judging that the tree outside the window cannot be the sum of so many cellulose molecules rests upon a premise that will not withstand critical scrutiny. If things were to turn out this way, then perhaps we could identify the tree with the sum of its molecular parts after all. So doing, perhaps we could be justified in rejecting both the Lockean view that the tree is a totally mysterious thing and the Russellian view that the tree is a bundle or collection of qualities.

Aristotle's argument appears to rest squarely upon certain intuitions concerning change and survival. Consider the tree case: We are assured that the same tree continues to exist outside my window from one year to the next. The tree is something that survives the loss of certain molecular components and the addition of other such components. Similarly, a comedy team or a football team continues to exist as individual people who "make up" the team are removed and replaced by new people. Over a period of time, a tree or a team may gradually undergo a *total* change of components. We can hardly identify either a tree or a team with the sum of individuals that are at any given time its parts, since in time this tree or team may be made up of entirely different parts. So we can hardly identify macroscopic things with collections of microscopic things.[19]

Is this assessment of the situation right? It is likely that some readers will doubt that it is. To decide whether this suspicion is well founded, we need to look more closely at the phenomenon of *change*. It is to the subject of change that we turn next.

CHAPTER 6

Change

A substance, as I shall use the term, is a "continuant" . . . something that can persist through time and can have different properties at different times.

SYDNEY SHOEMAKER, IDENTITY, CAUSE AND MIND (1984)[1]

A change, then, is a thing having incompatible different properties at different times.

D. H. MELLOR, REAL TIME (1981)[2]

6.1 An Analysis of Material Substance

Moore argues that there are "two classes of things," namely, "material objects" and "acts of consciousness." As was noted already, this seems to leave a good deal out. It seems that acts of consciousness take place in the *mind.* Surely our world contains *minds.* Why does Moore's inventory of what there is—Moore's *ontology*—make no mention of mind? One possible answer is that minds fall under the category of "material object." I am inclined to take this proposal seriously, for reasons suggested in Chapter 3. Moore disagrees, telling us that "no mind, and no act of consciousness can be a material object."[3] This leaves us with new problems. What sort of thing could a mind be if not a *material* thing? If we agree with Moore's view that minds are not material, we may conclude that the world contains both *material* things and *immaterial* things. If minds are not material things, what could minds be other than immaterial things?

　　I think we do well not to pursue further questions concerning the nature of the mind until we have a firmer grasp of what a *material* substance is. (We can hardly decide whether minds are material substances unless we know what sort of thing a material substance is.) Precisely what are we talking about when we make reference to material substances? It might be proposed that material substances are things that are independent of minds, things that can in theory continue to exist in circumstances in which no mind or minds exist. This proposal quickly encounters problems. If minds are themselves material substances, then it is hard to see how material substances can be independent of mind. Obviously nothing can exist in circumstances in which it fails to exist. No mind can exist independent of itself. So if minds are material entities, some material substances—namely minds—cannot exist independent of minds.

We might take a different tack and argue that anything that has a location in space and time (space-time) qualifies as a material substance. This sounds plausible when applied to garden variety objects such as the oak tree outside my window. Since this tree can be located in space-time, this tree qualifies as a material substance. In this respect the tree is not like the number 5. The number 5 is not located outside my window. Indeed, 5 does not appear to have *any* spatial location at all. If there is such a thing as the number 5, it seems that 5 fails to qualify as a material substance.

We seem to be on the right track. Unfortunately it may be argued that our revised analysis of material substance is still defective because it forces us to say that certain things that are *not* material substances *are* material substances. Consider the pile of dirty laundry that is presently in my closet. This pile of laundry has a certain spatiotemporal location; it exists in certain spatial locations for certain intervals of time. If everything that can be located in space-time is a material substance, my pile of dirty laundry qualifies as a material substance. But is that so? Is a pile of dirty laundry really a genuine *substance*? Followers of both Leibniz and Aristotle will deny this. And there is an interesting argument in behalf of their denial. Some stage setting is required before the argument in question can be set forth. In particular, we need to look at different ways in which things can undergo change.

6.2 Two Kinds of Change

Things change. It is a corollary of this plain fact that our knowledge of the world around us is in constant danger of being outdated. It may be true one moment but not the next that there is a cat in the closet or a psychopath at the bar. Change is itself a pervasive and notable feature of the world we inhabit. No theorist who hopes to give an accurate, general account of the way the world is can ignore the topic of change. As we shall see, this topic is closely tied to the task of understanding substantial things. On one interpretation of his position, Aristotle's analysis of substance is based largely upon certain facts concerning change.

What happens when a change occurs? We might judge that every change involves an annihilation. Gretchen is happy one minute, sad the next. Gretchen's happiness perishes, ceases to be, in this temporal period. Generalizing on this, we might conclude that every change involves an ending or annihilation of something. Is that so? Pranksters sneak into the firehouse and paint the fire truck navy blue. Here something—a certain fire truck—is first red and later blue. Does anything *perish*, cease to be, here? Certainly it does not seem correct to say that the truck itself perishes when the pranksters do their work. The truck might be annihilated if terrorists detonated a powerful bomb, but surely the truck is not destroyed when it changes color.

It might seem that the redness of the truck perishes, is annihilated, when the pranksters apply the new paint. (The color red does not perish; but perhaps the particular redness in this particular truck does.) The situation is much the same in the case of Gretchen changing from happy to sad. Gretchen does not perish in this process. But *something* perishes, namely, Gretchen's happiness—a certain state or condition of Gretchen. Clearly the color of a fire truck or the emotional condition of a person do not qualify as substantial things. The redness of the fire truck is somehow "in" the truck; the happiness of Gretchen somehow "in" Gretchen. Perhaps there is truth in the claim that every change involves the annihilation of something. But even if this is so, it does not follow that every change must involve the annihilation of a *substantial thing*. Gretchen's happiness perishes, ceases to exist, when she gets a certain phone call. But since Gretchen's happiness is not a substance, we cannot conclude that any substance perishes in the process.

A *substantial change* occurs when some substance—some substantial thing—either begins to exist (begins to be) or ceases to exist (ceases to be). A *qualitative change* occurs when some substantial thing changes qualitatively: this thing is first in one state or condition and subsequently in some different state or condition. Many theorists would argue that qualitative change occurs but substantial change does not when Gretchen undergoes an emotional change from being happy to being sad. A certain nonsubstantial thing, Gretchen's happiness, perishes in the process. But since no substance begins or ceases to be the change is merely qualitative and not substantial.

The situation may appear quite different when we consider the case of a terrorist's bomb. One minute the fire truck is sitting on the corner, and the next—an explosion having ripped the truck apart—it seems to have disappeared. Here it is natural to judge that a certain substantial thing—a fire truck—undergoes a substantial and not merely a qualitative change. It is not that the truck is in one state or condition before the explosion and in another state or condition afterward. It is, rather, that there *is* a truck one minute and there *is no truck* the next. The truck case seems entirely different from the Gretchen case. There *is* a Gretchen both before and after Gretchen's emotional transformation, but it is *not* true that there is a truck both before and after the terrorist's bomb explodes.

6.3   Dirty Laundry

A *mereological* change takes place whenever something loses or gains one or more parts (or both gains and loses parts). In many cases it seems that mereological change is a variety—one of many varieties—of *qualitative* change. Since things that change qualitatively in a temporal interval exist throughout this interval, mereological change is not substantial change. It seems that many things that undergo mereological change do not thereby perish—cease to exist—but are rather in one state or condition at one time and in another state or condition at a later time.

Imagine that the tree outside my window loses a leaf in the interval from t_1 to t_2. Since the tree remains otherwise the same, it certainly seems plausible that the tree *survives* the loss of a single leaf. This appears to be an example of a mereological change: something (the tree) first exists having leaf L as one of its parts and later exists lacking L as a part. Since the subject of change does not perish in the course of such a mereological change, it seems that some mereological changes are not substantial changes.

Followers of Aristotle argue that the capacity to undergo mereological change is one distinctive feature of genuine substances. An oak tree is not only something that exists independently of minds and has a certain location in space and time but also something that can—and in the normal course of things does—undergo mereological changes. When we are dealing with substances other than minds themselves, each of these requirements is arguably *necessary* for having the status of a material substance. Anything that satisfies all three requirements appears to be a material substance. The three requirements are individually necessary and jointly sufficient for being a material substance.

Now consider—if you can bear the spectacle—my pile of dirty laundry. Does such a thing qualify as a material substance? The answer is that it does not. The basis for this assessment of the situation is that a pile of dirty laundry is not something that can undergo mereological changes. When even a single dirty sock or shirt is removed or added to a previously existing pile of dirty laundry, we are left with a *new*, numerically different pile of dirty laundry that takes the place of the original pile.[4] It is not that the original pile of laundry continues to exist one sock or shirt the poorer or richer (thereby changing qualitatively). It is, rather, that we are confronted by *one* pile of dirty laundry at the beginning of the story and still *another* (different) pile of laundry at its end. The case involves a substantial change in which some pile of dirty laundry perishes or begins to exist. Since a mereological change is a qualitative change, the case is not properly described as one in which some enduring or persisting thing changes mereologically or persists through a change of parts.

Undoubtedly some people will be unconvinced by this. These people may ask why, if trees can survive (exist through) mereological changes, piles of dirty laundry cannot. It is a reasonable question. Though I cannot here give the question the full attention it deserves, let me say something in support of the view that piles of dirty laundry cannot survive mereological changes.

Try to suppose the contrary. Suppose, that is, that my pile of dirty laundry *can* survive the loss and addition of socks and various items of clothing. To simplify matters, let us imagine that the pile we start with at time t_1 is made up of precisely three dirty socks (S1, S2, and S3). At time t_2, we remove S3 and replace it by a new dirty sock (S4). Later, at time t_3, we replace sock S2 by another new dirty sock (S5). Finally, at time t_4, we replace sock S1 by still another dirty sock (S6). The situation thus looks like this:

Time t_1: Pile A (made up of S1, S2, S3)
Time t_2: Pile B (made up of S1, S2, S4)
Time t_3: Pile C (made up of S1, S5, S4)
Time t_4: Pile D (made up of S6, S5, S4)

Assuming (as we presently are) that piles of dirty laundry can undergo mereological change, it seems (1) that we can identify pile A and pile B, (2) that we can identify pile B and pile C, and (3) that we can identify pile C and pile D. If each of these identifications is correct, then it must be true that (4) we can correctly identify pile A and pile D. In short, our present assumptions commit us to saying that pile of laundry A (the one we started out with) and pile of laundry D (the one we wind up with) are one and the same pile of dirty laundry—a thing that changes qualitatively but not substantially in the t_1 to t_4 period. If our present assumptions are indeed correct, the situation is such that one and the same pile of dirty laundry is made up of entirely different parts or components at different times.

But is this really so? Suppose that a moment after t_4 we reunite socks S1, S2, S3 in a pile (pile E). Is pile E not the pile of dirty laundry that we started off with (pile A)? It seems that it is. Since pile E is not pile D (the two piles may exist side by side shortly after t_4), it seems that it cannot be right to identify pile A and pile D after all. Since the assumption that piles of laundry can undergo mereological change leads to the (mistaken) view that pile D *is* pile A, we thus have reason to question the view that piles of dirty laundry can undergo mereological change.

Granted, the argument proceeds quickly and is not easy to follow. If you have difficulty understanding this argument, it may not be a bad idea to find six dirty socks and run through a real-life version of the sequence of events depicted above. Undoubtedly some people who perform this experiment will still judge that the argument (not just the socks) has an unpleasant odor. I disagree with this. I think the argument just outlined is perfectly correct.

6.4   Idealism Revisited

As we saw earlier, Aristotle and his followers argue that we are not speaking of *matter* at all when we speak of the tree outside the window or the dog sleeping on the hearth. But then what *can* we be speaking of? One possible reply—it is important to recognize that it certainly is not Aristotle's reply—is that we are speaking of things that somehow are in, or dependent on, the mind. If the tree outside my window cannot be identified with the collection or sum of cellulose molecules outside the window, then it might be doubted that the tree can be a material thing. But if that is so, perhaps things turn out for the tree the way some people think things turn out for the mind. If minds are not material things, as Moore says, then must not minds be *immaterial* things? Similarly, if trees are not material things, must not trees be immaterial things? Assuming that immaterial things either are themselves minds or things that exist "in the mind," it might appear that Aristotle's denial that a tree can be identified with matter leads inevitably to the *idealist* position that trees are immaterial things existing in the mind.

It was argued in Chapter 2 that idealism should be rejected. If Aristotle's denial that trees are properly identified with sums of molecules really were to lead to an idealist assessment of trees, I think we would be justified in questioning Aristotle's position. In fact, however, Aristotle and his followers are *not* committed to idealism. So the arguments opposing idealism do not carry any weight in opposition to Aristotle's position.

Indeed, Aristotelian arguments opposing the proposal that the tree outside my window can properly be identified with the collection of cellulose molecules outside my window can easily be extended so as to oppose the idealist view that the tree can properly be identified with a collection of *ideas.* If we identify the tree with any particular collection of molecules, then (since this collection of molecules perishes when even a single constituent molecule is added or taken away) the *tree* itself must perish when even a single molecule is added or taken away. Since Aristotle denies that the tree *does* perish when a single molecule is added or taken away, he concludes that the tree cannot properly be identified with any collection of molecules. Precisely the same argument might be used in opposition to the strange view that my tree is a collection of ideas— say, the collection of ideas I presently have when I view the tree. Take away even one constituent idea, and you are left with a *new* collection of ideas (the original collection perishing in the process). Since the tree itself clearly persists—continues to exist—as individual ideas (or sensations) come and go, an Aristotelian will conclude that the tree cannot properly be identified either with a collection of molecules or a collection of ideas. As a substance, the tree outside my window persists or endures in a way that no mere *collection* (aggregate, bundle) of things persists or endures. So the tree outside my window cannot properly be identified with any collection whatsoever, whether it be a collection of "spiritual" or "material" things.

Aristotle would *not* deny that there is a collection of cellulose molecules located outside my window. He *would* deny that any tree can correctly be identified with this sum of molecules. As I have said already, Aristotle is not thereby committed to judging that any tree exists in any mind or is dependent upon any mind for its existence. A tree is a *material substance,* something that is located in space-time, is independent of minds, and can (and in the normal course of things will) survive mereological changes. The tree does not perish—is not replaced by a *new* tree—when a leaf or a molecule is lost or added. There is nothing here to give comfort to Berkeley and his followers. When we deny that we are speaking of any particular aggregate or mass of matter—any particular sum or collection of molecules or microscopic entities—in referring to material substances such as an oak tree, we need not thereby commit ourselves to the implausible view that oak trees exist in minds or that they are mind-dependent entities.

Some people are profoundly suspicious of the Aristotelian position. Is it not plainly absurd to judge that *two* material things—a collection of cellulose molecules and an oak tree—are presently located in precisely the same place outside my window? No doubt different material things can occupy the same place at *different* times. But how can two things occupy the same spatial position at the same time?

In considering this objection, we should distinguish between two *exclusion principles* (as they might be called):

(E1) It is impossible for two things to be located in the same place at the same time.

(E2) It is impossible for two things of the same kind to be located in the same place at the same time.

Principle (E2) is very plausible. Certainly it is hard to conceive of two bowling balls, cats, or trees occupying precisely the same spatial location at the same time. But note that (E2) does not imply (E1). Even if (E2) is true, it might be the case that things of different kinds coexist in the sense of occupying the same position at the same time. If the argument outlined above is sound, (E1) is false even though (E2) is true. The tree that exists outside my window is a material substance, though the collection of molecules that exists outside the window is not. Since we cannot *identify* the tree with the collection of molecules, we are here dealing with *two* things that presently coexist. But this is not a counterexample to principle (E2), since a tree and a collection of molecules are not the same kind of thing (the former being and the latter failing to be a material substance).

In brief, the Aristotelian position is something like this: Trees are material substances and not collections of ideas located in any mind. Nor is a tree a collection of molecules or microscopic entities. Every tree coexists with but is distinct from a collection of cellulose molecules. Aristotle's denial that a tree can be identified with its matter turns on the claim that a tree survives or endures—continues to exist—as its molecular constituents or parts come and go. The same thing cannot be said of any collection or sum of molecules. Like piles of dirty laundry, collections of molecules are simply incapable of surviving mereological change. (The argument opposing mereological change in the case of my pile of dirty laundry can be extended to oppose the suggestion that the same collection of cellulose molecules is capable of undergoing mereological change.) It is this fact that disqualifies collections of molecules from being genuine material substances in Aristotle's sense. Collections of molecules do not survive mereological change in the manner of genuine substances and so cannot be genuine substances.

6.5   Can We Step into the Same River Twice?

The Greek philosopher Heraclitus argued that we cannot step into the same river twice. Since the river into which I step one minute has different molecular constituents from the river into which I step the next, the former is different from the latter—and so not "the same" river as the latter. If we follow Aristotle's lead, we will reject this reasoning as involving a number of mistakes. From the fact that I do not step into the same collection of water molecules on the two occasions in question it does not follow that I do not step into the same river on each occasion. Each alteration in molecular constituents leaves us with a different river-shaped collection of molecules. Since such mereological alterations are constantly occurring, we cannot step into the same river-shaped collection of molecules on two occasions. Since river-shaped collections of molecules are not rivers, it does not follow from this that we cannot step into the same river on two occasions.

Granted, it may sound strange to say that the collection of water molecules that coexists with a river is not itself a river. But here we must exercise caution. In one sense of "is," it is true that a river-shaped collection of water molecules *is* a river. In still another sense of "is," this is false. We might call the first "is" the "is" of *composition* and the second the "is" of *identity.* It is perfectly true that one collection of molecules is/composes a river one minute and still another collection of molecules is/composes this same river the next minute. Similarly for oak trees, cats, and basketball teams: one collection of cellulose molecules is/composes my tree one day and still another collection is/composes the same tree the next day. What is *not* true is that one collection of molecules is identical with the tree (river) one day and still another collection of molecules is identical with the same tree the next day. Thus it is important that we appreciate the difference between the "is" of composition and the "is" of identity. If X composes Y, then X and Y are not one (the same) thing. If X is identical with Y, then X and Y are one (the same) thing.[5]

Suppose that a sculptor takes a certain piece of clay (C) and creates a lovely and valuable statue (S). At the outset of the story it is not true that clay C is a statue, while at the conclusion of the story it *is* true. Obviously statue S does not yet *exist* at the outset of the story. Since C exists before S does, C and S are *discernible* in the sense that something that is true of C is not true of S.

C and S would be *indiscernible* only in the event that everything that is true of C is true of S, and conversely. As we have just seen, this is not the case. Certain things that are true of C fail to be true of S. For example, it is true that C exists before the sculptor creates S but not true that S exists before he creates S. Clay C and statue S thus fail to be indiscernible. Even though C and S coexist after the creation process is completed, C and S are discernible.

This means that we cannot say that C is identical with S. Identity requires indiscernibility (the principle of the indiscernibility of identity). Since C exists before S does, C and S fail to be indiscernible and so fail to be *identical.* Identity claims hold when and only when we can correctly identify "one" thing with "another" thing.

But correct identification never occurs in cases where we encounter things that are discernible. We cannot identify Mark Twain as the author of *Moby Dick* precisely because things that are true of Twain fail to be true of the author of *Moby Dick*. We cannot identify clay C and statue S—even when C and S coexist—since things that are true of C fail to be true of S and things that are true of S fail to be true of C. Thus, in one sense, we speak falsely if we say that clay C is statue S. It is false that C is identical with S. (C is one thing, S another.) In another sense, we speak truly when we say that C is S: C does compose S. Much as a club or a team may be *composed of* different people at different times, it may be true at one time that one collection of molecules is/composes a certain river and true at another time that still another collection of molecules is/composes this same river. To say that a collection of molecules is/composes a river at time *t* is to say, in effect, that the various molecules that make up this collection qualify as constituents or parts of the river in question at time *t*. Note that the "is" of composition does not require indiscernibility. Since rivers persist or endure through time in a way that collections of water molecules do not, no river is such that it is indiscernible with any collection of water molecules. It is true that the Colorado River existed ten (or a hundred) years ago, but not true that the collection of water molecules that presently coexists with the Colorado River existed ten (or a hundred) years ago. From the fact that the river is discernible from the collection of molecules with which it presently coexists, Aristotelians conclude that it is not true that this collection of molecules is identical with (the same thing as) the Colorado River. The collection cannot, though the river can, survive mereological changes.

6.6   Further Questions

All this leaves us with a number of unanswered questions. We have seen that *quantities of matter* (collections of molecules) are/compose material substances. Can it also happen that *material substances* are/compose material substances? If we think that the expression "the president" names a single enduring material substance in each of the following statements,

> Washington is (was) the president in 1778.
>
> Jefferson is (was) the president in 1802.

> Wilson is (was) the president in 1915.
> Reagan is (was) the president in 1988.

we may answer in the affirmative. Obviously Washington, Jefferson, Wilson, and Reagan are different individuals. Different individuals cannot be *identical* with one thing. (Two people cannot be identified with one person.) Conceivably it might be thought that the operative "is" in the four statements above is properly interpreted as the "is" of composition. Much as different collections of molecules can at different times be/compose one tree, it might be suspected that different people can at different times be/compose one official (the president). On this view, the president persists or endures (survives) from 1778 through 1988, different individuals (people) being/composing the president at different times. Assuming that people are material substances, it appears that different material substances are/compose a single material substance at different times.[6]

I doubt that this assessment of the matter is correct. My guess is that the term "the president" does not designate a single substance that exists both in 1778 and 1988. Rather, this expression picks out one individual in 1778 and yet another, numerically different individual in 1988. The individual who answers to "the president" in 1988 once was employed as a radio broadcaster for baseball games. Since this is not true of the individual who answered to "the president" in 1778, these individuals (Washington and Reagan) are not indiscernible and so not identical.

But could we not say that Washington and Reagan are two individuals who at different times compose the enduring substance that is the president? If this proposal is correct, then it seems that substances (and not just collections of molecules and microscopic entities) sometimes compose substances. Why should this proposal not be correct?

The answer lies, I think, with an exclusion principle considered earlier, namely:

(E2) It is impossible for two things of the same kind to be located in the same place at the same time.

If we say in 1986 that the president is a man, we speak truly. We also speak truly when we say of Reagan in 1988 that he is a man. If Reagan merely composed the president in 1988, then there would be not one but *two* things (Reagan and the president) who are in

1988 located in the same places at the same times. Since Reagan is a man and the president is a man, that would mean that two individuals *of the same kind* are located in the same place at the same time. This conflicts with principle (E2). If (E2) is correct, as I think it is, then we should reject the view that different individuals compose an enduring substance called "the president." The expression "the president" designates different individuals in 1778 and 1988 and so does not designate one enduring substance that exists throughout the 1778–1988 period.

Some people will argue, in a Heraclitean spirit, that the expression "the tree outside my window" is like "the president" with respect to the fact that it picks out different things (different collections of molecules) at different times. I doubt that this is right. No collection of molecules can survive mereological changes. Since trees can—and in the normal course of things do—survive such changes, we are not speaking of collections of molecules when we employ expressions such as "the tree outside my window."

While the latter expression designates a substantial thing that persists or endures from one day or one decade to the next, the former expression does not designate such a substantial thing. Accordingly, the president case does not establish that different material substances may at different times compose a single material substance. I doubt that any case will serve to establish this.

Material substances are thus not collections of ideas, qualities, or even molecules. No collection of things persists or endures through mereological changes in the manner of a genuine material substance. As a material substance, the tree outside my window coexists with—is composed of—different collections of cellulose molecules at different times. Unlike a collection of molecules or a pile of dirty laundry, a tree undergoes a qualitative and not a substantial change when one of its parts is removed and replaced by a new part. Numerically speaking, the tree that is outside my window today and the tree that was outside it one year ago are the same tree. Qualitatively speaking, they are, to be sure, different. (The former is taller than the latter.) But one material substance can at different times be in different qualitative states.

Are people material substances? As we might expect, there is sharp disagreement about this. In addressing the issue, we are naturally led to ask what sorts of changes a person can and cannot survive. It is to this subject that we will turn next.

CHAPTER 7

Personal Identity

I weigh more than three pounds, am more than six inches high. . . . But the brain is the only part of me whose destruction I could not possibly survive.

THOMAS NAGEL, *THE VIEW FROM NOWHERE* (1986)[1]

7.1 Matter and Form

A person's history extends from the time he or she first exists to the moment at which he or she perishes. There is some controversy when it comes to the task of locating the times at which people begin to exist and cease to exist. For the moment let us focus on beginnings. When did I first exist? Some people will judge that I first existed at the time of my birth. Others, contesting this, will argue that I first exist—nine months or so before my birth—at the time of my conception. Is either view correct? We may doubt that we can make much progress with the question until we have a precise analysis of what sort of thing I am.[2] How can we hope to track or follow the history or career of something unless we first know what kind of thing we are dealing with?

    It is easy to compile a list of things I am not. I am not an idea in any mind, not a quality, not a collection of living cells. I am a substantial thing. But what does *that* mean? Followers of Aristotle say

> A Substance is an enduring entity which is, in a sense, a compound of matter and form (though these two are not *parts* of the Substance). Its matter is what the Substance is made of, its form is what is specified by an answer to the question "what is it to be that thing?"[3]

My matter changes from day to day. (Different collections of cells are located where I am located from one day to the next.) Aristotelians deny that the same thing can be said of my "form." But exactly what is my "form," anyway? We are told that a thing's form is "what we describe when we answer the question 'what is it to be a thing of that kind?' "[4] But this brings us back to the question: What kind of thing am I?

We might despair of giving a uniquely correct answer to such a question. Many different terms, representing many different kinds of things, correctly apply to me. Does this not suggest that I have not one form but many forms? I am not one but rather many kinds of thing.

Aristotle and his followers will argue that this way of looking at the matter involves a confusion. It is true that the term "teacher" applies to me—and to many other individuals as well. Nonetheless, "teacher" is not a term that stands for a genuine—or as some theorists say *natural*—kind of thing. Those of us who are teachers might very well have existed without ever being teachers. Being a teacher is not part of what is involved in being me, since I might very well exist as a nonteacher.[5] To learn what kind of thing I really am, we need to locate a general term that applies to me *essentially*—that is, roughly, a term that must apply to me at any time at which I exist. Terms such as "teacher" and "softball player" fail to explain what kind of thing I really am, since such terms might very well *not* have applied to me at all.

Some theorists maintain that the situation is quite different when we turn from "teacher" to "person." Both terms apply to a great many individuals. But there may appear to be an important difference between the two terms. No individual who is a teacher *had* to be a teacher. (Each such individual might have existed as something other than a teacher.) Arguably the situation is not like this at all when we turn to "person." It is hard, at least, to imagine any individual who *is* a person existing as something other than a person. Jane Fonda could not have existed as, say, a bowling ball or a skyscraper, just as I could not have existed as a cloud or a tree. People are *essentially* people, though teachers are not *essentially* teachers. When we locate what an individual is essentially—what it could not fail to be—we in effect locate its *form* and so know what kind of thing we are dealing with.

7.2   Do We Exist When We Are Born?

If this is correct, my "form" consists of being a person. But this leaves us with the question: What is involved in being a person? This is another large question that can be addressed only briefly here. Michael Tooley says:

> There is . . . considerable disagreement about what it is that makes something a person. All of the answers that survive even mild scrutiny, however, agree at least on this: the relevant features are *psychological* in nature. Something is a person by virtue of the sort of mental life that it enjoys. . . .[6]

The fertilized egg from which a person develops has no mental life and so, on Tooley's analysis, fails to be a person. Since each of us (each person) has the form of a person, it follows that none of us can correctly be identified with the fertilized egg from which we developed. On this view, I fail to exist shortly after my conception for the same sorts of reasons that an oak tree fails to exist at the time when the acorn from which it develops falls to the ground. Since an acorn is not a tree, we cannot say that the tree presently outside my window once existed as an acorn. Things work the same way when we turn from trees to people. Since a fertilized egg (zygote) is not a person, no person can be identified with any fertilized egg.

This result might encourage those who say that we first exist when we are born (and not when we are conceived). But is this really so? Tooley argues that even a newborn infant fails to be a person, saying that it is

> . . . extraordinarily unlikely that the cerebral cortex of a human, within a week or so after birth, contains the necessary physical basis of those psychological states and capacities that are essential if something is to be a person.[7]

If Tooley is right about this, something seems to go wrong with the proposal that I am a substance whose form (or essence) is being a person. Surely I exist at the time of my birth. (It cannot be "my" birth otherwise. But whose birth can it possibly be, if not mine?) But if so—if I do exist at the time when I am born—it does not appear that any *psychological* features can be essential features of me (since I exist at certain times lacking such features). If, as Tooley conjectures, being a *person* is a matter of having the status of a psychological being, then I exist at certain times as a nonperson. So it simply cannot be right to say that my essence or form is specified by "person."

7.3 Secular Resurrection

However, it might be objected that newborn infants and even about-to-be-born individuals (fetuses) can feel pain and hunger. Perhaps such beings have psychological features and so qualify as persons, contrary to Tooley. Perhaps it is true after all that my essence or form is to be a person.

Descartes, among others, seems to subscribe to such a view. Descartes argues that *consciousness* is something of which he cannot "be deprived."

> I am, I exist; that is certain. For how long? For as long as I am experiencing . . . if I wholly ceased from experiencing, I should at once wholly cease to be.[8]

For Descartes, it is not sensory experience but *thought* that is essential to a person's continued existence. This theme is closely tied to Descartes's conviction that he is not logically dependent upon his *body* for his continued existence. Many religious people judge that it is not only possible but *true* that they will go on existing following their biological death and following, too, the destruction of their bodies. If this assumption of an "afterlife" is true, then a person is not the same thing as the object that is his or her body. (If A can exist in circumstances where B does not exist, then A is not the same thing as B.) The challenge is to show, or provide good reasons for believing, that we do continue to exist, perhaps in "heaven" or in "hell," after our bodies have been transformed to dust. It is indeed a formidable challenge.

The beauty of Descartes's position is that the argument does not rest upon the questionable assumption that there *is* an afterlife. At present Jack is sitting on the sofa reading a newspaper. Located precisely where Jack is located is a certain human *body*. Descartes would argue that it is a mistake to judge that this body, Jack's body, *is* Jack. But Descartes would not base his argument upon the assumption that Jack *will* continue to exist after his body perishes. His argument is based upon the much more modest assumption that it is, in theory, *possible* that Jack will continue to exist after his body dies. It is not possible for Jack's body—the body that is presently located on the sofa—to go on existing after it, this same body, perishes. (A thing perishes when it perishes.) If it is merely *possible* for Jack, the person sitting on the sofa, to go on existing after Jack's body perishes, then something is true of Jack that is not true of Jack's body—which means that Jack cannot *be* Jack's body. Clearly A and B cannot be identified if something that is possible for A is not possible for B.

We might construct an argument, entirely noncommital concerning religious assumptions, for the Cartesian conclusion that it is possible for Jack (a certain person) to go on existing after his body has perished. Derek Parfit suggests as much. Parfit believes that it is in theory possible that a remarkable machine called a Teletransporter will one day be invented that enables ordinary people to go on living after their original bodies are destroyed.

> I enter the Teletransporter. . . . This machine will send me at the speed of light. . . . When I press the button, I shall lose consciousness, and then wake up at what seems a moment later. In fact I shall have been unconscious for about an hour. The Scanner here on Earth will destroy my brain and body, while recording the exact states of all my cells. It will then transport this information by radio. Travelling at the speed of light, the message will take three minutes to reach the Replicator on Mars. This will then create, out of new matter, a brain and a body exactly like mine. It will be in this body that I shall wake up.[9]

Note that Parfit would not agree with the passage cited at the outset of this chapter. He would reject the claim that even Jack's brain is essential to Jack's continued existence. It is possible that someday Teletransporters will be commonplace. So it is possible that someday Jack will step into a Teletransporter in Boston and shortly thereafter appear in Seattle with a new body and even a new brain. Jack's original body may in this way perish long before Jack himself perishes. So Jack cannot be identified with the body that is presently located where Jack is located.

7.4 Psychological Connectedness

Let us call the person who steps into the Scanner in Boston "Jack B" and the one who shortly thereafter steps out of the Replicator in Seattle "Jack S." Can it really be true that Jack S *is* Jack B? Can it be true that Jack S, the person who turns up in Seattle, is the same person as Jack B? Jack S may not look much like Jack B. Indeed, Jack S may be physically entirely different from the person who earlier stepped into the Scanner in Boston. Since Jack S and Jack B have different fingerprints, the FBI no doubt would conclude that they are different people. If the FBI's appraisal of the matter is correct, Parfit's story about the Teletransporter fails to establish that it is possible for a person to continue living with a "new" body and brain.

But is the FBI right? I doubt that the fingerprint test settles the matter. For consider the possibility that both Jack's hands are horribly and irreparably damaged by a chain saw. In these days of medical miracles, it is in theory possible for a team of specialists to successfully carry out a "double hand" transplant, a recently deceased person's hands being transplanted to Jack's body. The person who emerges from the hospital is none other than *Jack*, this despite the fact that this person does not have the same fingerprints as the person whose hands were earlier destroyed by the chain saw. Obviously the same person may go on existing with different hands and new fingerprints. The FBI test does not establish that Jack S is not the same person as Jack B.

Indeed, perhaps there is good reason to judge that Jack S is the same person as Jack B. Psychologically speaking, Jack S is remarkably like Jack B. In particular, Jack S seems to remember, in incredible detail, doing things that only Jack B once did. This fact prompts some theorists to conclude that Jack S is the same person as Jack B. Suppose that Jack S really remembers striking out with the bases loaded in the ninth inning of a certain baseball game that was played ten years before Jack B stepped into the Scanner. If we discover that Jack B is the person who struck out in the ninth inning in the game in question, it is hard to see how we cannot conclude that Jack S is the same person as Jack B. How can one person remember doing something done by *another* person? We may well judge this to be impossible. So if we are convinced that Jack S *does* remember striking out on the occasion when Jack B struck out, we may conclude that Jack S is Jack B.

Some people believe that it is in theory possible for a person to exist "in one life" with one body and later to be reincarnated and exist in "another life" with still another body. If reincarnation is a genuine possibility, then it is in theory possible for a person I meet today to *be* Napoleon, the man who was defeated at the Battle of Waterloo in 1815. Could there conceivably be any reason to judge that such a remarkable thing actually happens? Well, perhaps. Suppose that a man we meet in a bar today really can recount, in incredible detail and with astonishing accuracy, countless events at the Battle of Waterloo. Suppose, too, it could be shown that this man has never read any books on the Battle of Waterloo or talked to historians who specialize in studying that battle. This situation is certainly not *impossible*. And if such a situation were to arise, we might well be tempted to conclude that the person we meet in the bar really was present at the Battle of Waterloo. We might judge that this person actually *remembers* making strategic decisions that were made by Napoleon nearly two hundred years ago.

We might say that a person who presently exists is *strongly connected,* psychologically speaking, to a person who previously existed if and only if the former remembers doing things only the latter did. On this analysis, I am not strongly connected to George Washington. Although I remember *that* Washington crossed the Delaware during the Revolutionary War, I do not remember *crossing* the Delaware at this time. Remembering that a certain historical figure acted in a certain way is no guarantee that I am strongly connected to this figure.

The situation would be entirely different if I could actually remember doing things only Washington once did. If I were strongly connected psychologically to Washington, it seems that I would *be* the same person as Washington. This is perhaps an illustration of what John Locke means when he observes:

> For it being the same consciousness that makes a man be himself to himself, personal identity depends on that only, whether it be annexed solely to one individual substance, or can be continued in a succession of several substances. For as far as any intelligent being can repeat the idea of any past action with the same consciousness it had of it at first . . . so far it is the same personal self.[10]

Locke seems to allow that it is in theory possible for the same consciousness to be "annexed" at different times to different "substances"—presumably different bodies. It is only when person A has the same consciousness as person B that it can truly be said that A is the same person as B. The fact that A has one body and B another body does not, for Locke, establish that A is not the same person as B. Conceivably A and B may have different bodies and also the same consciousness. In such a case, A is the same as B.

What is involved in having the same consciousness? Locke might be interpreted in a number of ways here. On one interpretation, he endorses the following principles:

(L1) A (who exists at present) is the same person as B (who existed at some previous time) if A is strongly connected, psychologically, to B.

(L2) A (who exists at present) is the same person as B (who existed at some previous time) only if A is strongly connected, psychologically, to B.

(L1) says that psychological connectedness involving memory is *sufficient*; it is a guarantee of personal identity. (L2) says something a bit different, namely, that psychological connectedness is *necessary*—required, if you will—for personal identity. Suppose that Jack suffers irreversible and total amnesia as a result of some neurological disorder at time *t*. (L2) implies, while (L1) does not imply, that the person who has Jack's body after time *t* is not Jack—is not the same person as Jack. Being the same person is a matter of having "the same consciousness," which on the present interpretation is a matter of strong psychological connectedness. If (L2) is true, the fact that person A has the same fingerprints as person B does not justify the conclusion that A is the same person as B.

7.5 The Brave Officer Argument

There is a famous objection to Locke's analysis of personal identity that was first presented in 1785 in Thomas Reid's work *Essays on the Intellectual Powers of Man*. Reid suggests the following:

> Suppose a brave officer to have been flogged when a boy at school for robbing an orchard, to have taken a standard from the enemy in his first campaign, and to have been made a general in advanced life; suppose, also, which must be admitted to be possible, that, when he took the standard, he was conscious of his having been flogged at school, and that, when made a general, he was conscious of his taking the standard, but had absolutely lost the consciousness of his flogging.[11]

Reid is here presenting materials for construction of the following argument opposing Locke's position: suppose that (L1) and (L2) were true. Since the officer who captures the enemy flag at time t_2 remembers being flogged for stealing apples at time t_1, principle (L1) tells us that the brave officer is the same person as the boy who earlier was flogged. Moreover, since the general remembers at time t_3 capturing the enemy flag at t_2, (L1) further tells us that the general is the same person as the brave officer. However, since the general does not remember being flogged at t_1—does not, let us suppose, remember anything about the life of the boy who is flogged either at or before the time of the flogging—principle (L2) implies that the general is not the same person as the boy who earlier was flogged. We thus are left with the following results:

(1) the general is the same person as the brave officer.
(2) the brave officer is the same person as the boy who was flogged.
(3) the general is not the same person as the boy who was flogged.

Are these three claims consistent? That is, can all three claims be true? Reid would deny this. Identity is a *transitive* relation in the sense that if A is identical to B and B, in turn, is identical to C, then A must be identical to C. In light of the transitivity of identity, Reid would argue that if (1) and (2) are true then (3) *must* be false. Since principle (L1) assures us that (1) and (2) are true, and principle (L2) assures us that (3) is true, Reid would conclude that (L1) and (L2) cannot both be correct. If principle (L2) is correct, then the general is not the same person as the boy who was flogged earlier—which means, contrary to principle (L1), that (1) and (2) cannot both be true. On the other hand, if (L1) is correct, then (1) and (2) are true, which implies that the general is the same person as the boy who was flogged. Since the general is not psychologically connected to this boy, principle (L2) must then be rejected. As Reid observes, Locke's analysis of personal identity must be rejected because it implies that "the general is, and at the same time is not, the same person with him who was flogged at school."

There are various things that might be said in defense of the Lockean position or something close to the Lockean position. Perhaps (L1) and (L2) are best interpreted as claims that do not concern *identity* at all. Recently Parfit has argued that we do best to "give up the language of identity" when we consider questions concerning the continued existence or *survival* of a person.[12] Conceivably followers of Locke might interpret (L1) and (L2) in terms not of personal identity but of personal survival. Thus:

(L1*) B (who existed at some time in the past) presently survives as A (a person who now exists) if A is strongly connected to B.

(L2*) B (who existed at some time in the past) presently survives as A (a person who now exists) only if A is strongly connected to B.

It might be argued that these revised principles do not come to grief when we consider Reid's case of the brave officer. Since survival does not require identity, we can grant that the brave officer survives as the general without saying that the brave officer is identical with the general. Similarly, we can judge that the boy who is punished survives as the brave officer without being committed to the view that the boy is identical to the officer. Statements (1), (2), and (3) are then interpreted in terms not of personal identity but only of a person's survival or continued existence. Perhaps survival is not transitive. If so, it can happen that C survives as B and that B survives as A and yet not happen that C survives as A. On the "survival" interpretation, it might be argued that statement (3) can be false even though (1) and (2) are true. As Parfit observes, identity is, but strong connectedness is not, a transitive relation.[13]

7.6   Is Survival Without Identity Possible?

Will the revised Lockean position then bear critical examination? I have doubts about this. For one thing, it is unclear that personal survival can be separated from personal identity. Suppose that the boy who is flogged survives as the brave officer who wins the enemy flag. If that is so, it certainly seems that the brave officer *is* the boy who was flogged. If we deny that the officer and the boy are *one* person—deny that the personal identity relation holds between the boy and the officer—it simply is not clear what can be made of the further claim that the boy continues to exist as the officer. How can the boy continue to exist as the officer if the officer is not the same person as the boy?

There is a further worry. Even if survival can be separated

from identity, as Parfit suggests, it is by no means clear that survival fails to be a transitive relation. Suppose that Napoleon, the man who directs the French army at the Battle of Waterloo, remembers doing something only Caesar once did—say, crossing the Rubicon at a certain time. Suppose, too, that the man presently in the bar remembers directing the French forces at Waterloo but does not remember crossing the Rubicon. (L1*) suggests that it then could have truly been said in 1815 that:

(1) Caesar presently survives as Napoleon.

The same principle implies that we presently can say that:

(2) Napoleon presently survives as the man at the bar.

However, principle (L2*) also tells us that:

(3) Caesar does not presently survive as the man at the bar.

But can all three statements really be true? If Caesar really "survives as" Napoleon in 1815, then presumably Napoleon *is* Caesar. But if Napoleon is Caesar, and Napoleon "survives as" the man presently in the bar, then must not the man in the bar *be* Caesar? Assuming that Caesar continues to exist as Napoleon and that Napoleon continues to exist as the man in the bar, it is hard to see how it can be denied that Caesar continues to exist as the man in the bar. In effect, defenders of principles (L1*) and (L2*) are faced with precisely the same sort of objection that Reid raised for defenders of (L1) and (L2). And we may doubt that there is a satisfactory reply to the objection in either case.

7.7   The Duplication Objection

For reasons noted already, Parfit's case of the Teletransporter might appear to establish that a person cannot be identified with the object that is her or his body. Does Reid's brave officer case show that this is not so? It seems not. At most, Reid's example shows that we cannot consistently accept both (L1) and (L2). Suppose that we were to accept (L1) and reject (L2). In that case we avoid Reid's problem entirely. And it appears that (L1) is all that is needed to establish that cases of teletransportation have the corollary that people are not their bodies.

To make this clearer, recall the previous example: Jack B steps into the Teletransporter (the Scanner) in Boston at one time. Shortly thereafter Jack S steps out of the Teletransporter (the Replicator) in Seattle. Jack B is thin and tall, Jack S is short and fat. Still, Jack S seems to remember doing many things that only Jack B previously did. Note that there is nothing mysterious or miraculous about the apparent fact that Jack S is strongly connected, psychologically speaking, to Jack B. After all, Jack S's brain is an exact duplicate of Jack B's brain. Given the incredible detail and accuracy of Jack S's reports concerning events in Jack B's life and the further fact that Jack S appears to remember these events in a first-person, "This happened to me" manner, we may be tempted to conclude that Jack S really does remember doing and suffering things only Jack B did and suffered. Given principle (L1), it then follows that Jack S is indeed the same person as Jack B. Jack B thus finds himself in Seattle after the teletransportation process is complete.

But Jack B's body, or perhaps one should say Jack B's *original* body, has perished at the time Jack S strolls down the street in Seattle. If we allow that the case of teletransportation is possible, it appears *possible* for a person to continue to exist after her or his (original) body has ceased to exist. Needless to say, this result is music to the ears of Descartes and his followers. If I can exist at a time when my (present) body has perished, then I cannot *be* my (present) body.

What, then, can I be if I am not my body? As we saw in Chapter 3, dualists will argue that I am a "partly physical system"—a compound thing that presently has a certain human body as one of its components and also has a certain spiritual entity (my mind) as another component. On this assessment of the situation, your arms and legs are material components while your *mind* is an immaterial component of the individual person that is you.[14] For reasons noted already (Chapter 3), I think we do well to resist this account of the situation. But if we are not to sign on with the dualists, how are we to respond to the apparent possibility of body switching?

Perhaps there is a way of allowing for body switching and also resisting dualism. Indeed, the roots of such a position might appear to be present in Aristotle's own work. Perhaps if we adopt "a naturalistic framework for understanding what it is to be a person," we can both allow that Jack S and Jack B are one person (located at different times) and also deny that the mind of this person is an immaterial entity.[15] The key point here is that, for Aristotelians, the mind is not a component *substance* but rather a *capacity* of certain individuals. As Peter Smith and O. R. Jones argue:

> [Aristotle] articulates the key idea that having a soul or mind is a question of one's capacities. From the perspective of this Aristotelian framework, the rival Cartesian supposition that the mind is a component of a person is diagnosed as a simple fallacy of . . . treating something's form as one of its constituents.[16]

The idea, briefly, is that having a mind is a matter of having the capacity to do certain things—for example, to solve problems, to remember things one has done, and to formulate plans. Since Jack S and Jack B have the same psychological capacities, we may judge not only that they have the same mind but that they are the same person. None of this commits us to the Cartesian thesis that some immaterial substance is a component of a person. Your mind is not a substantial *thing* but rather a cluster of psychological capacities. Thus we can have it both ways, allowing the possibility of switching bodies and also rejecting dualism.

I think we may be on the right track here. Still, I have reservations concerning teletransportation. Many people judge from such cases that it is in theory possible for a person's mind to be transferred from one body to another. If this possibility were to be realized, it seems you would continue to exist if your mind were transported into a new body. The argument does not rest on any beliefs concerning supernatural beings or an afterlife in heaven or hell. The argument rests upon principle (L1) and the more modest assumption that an individual having a brain that is an exact duplicate of your brain would be psychologically connected to you. (Reid's brave officer story poses no threat to this position.)

There is, however, a potential problem. Suppose, for the sake of argument, that (L1) is true. Suppose also that the Teletransporter makes not one but *two* copies of Jack's original brain. In this case *two* people, Jack S1 and Jack S2, emerge from the Replicator in Seattle. Obviously it cannot be true both that Jack S1 is Jack B and that Jack S2 is Jack B. Two individuals cannot be one individual. This suggests that principle (L1) must be rejected. Since principle (L1) tells us that two people are identical with one person—which is impossible—(L1) must itself be rejected.[17]

Perhaps it helps to pose the story in terms of responsibility.

Jack B borrows $10 from Jill before the teletransportation process begins. Later Jill encounters two people, Jack S1 and Jack S2, each of whom seems to remember borrowing the money from Jill. Can Jill correctly say that only Jack S1 owes her $10? Something seems wrong with this, since Jack S2 has precisely as much claim to being Jack B as does Jack S1. It would be entirely arbitrary to hold Jack S1 but not Jack S2 responsible for paying back the money. It would be equally arbitrary to hold Jack S2 and not Jack S1 responsible.

It might be suggested that both survivors should be held responsible. But there is a real problem with this proposal. How can *two* people be responsible for performing the previous deeds of a single person? Jack S1 does not owe Jill the money unless Jack S1 is Jack B, the person who borrowed the money from Jill. Similarly for Jack S2. The problem is that it simply cannot be true both that Jack S1 is the person who borrowed the money and that Jack S2 is the person who borrowed the money. We cannot employ duplication techniques of teletransportation to ensure that Jill has a right to a $20 return on a $10 loan.

One way—indeed, perhaps the most plausible way—of resolving the problem is by denying that either Jack S1 or Jack S2 really is the person who borrowed the money from Jill. In that case, Jack S1 and Jack S2 are mere replicas of, and not identical with, Jack B. Neither of these Jack replicas owes Jill $10, since neither *is* the person who borrowed the money from Jill. Since both survivors appear to be psychologically connected to Jack B and since neither survivor really is the same person as Jack B, we should reject principle (L1).

However, once (L1) goes, the teletransportation case offers no comfort to those who hope to establish that it is possible for a person to continue to exist after his body has perished. Teletransportation cases establish merely that it is possible that a *replica* of any presently existing person may exist in the future at a time when this person's body has perished. So what? From the fact that a *replica* of myself will exist a hundred years from now, after my present body has perished, it does not follow that *I* can exist after my present body has perished. (The replica might very well fool people—but the fact remains it simply is not the real thing.) We will have to do better than this if we hope to establish that we can exist after our bodies cease to exist.

7.8   Death

Needless to say, I think that the Aristotelian rejection of the (Cartesian) proposal that minds are immaterial substances is well motivated. At the same time, I have doubts concerning the Aristotelian theme that both of the following statements are true:

(A) The form (essence) of individual people is to be a person.

(B) Being a person is something that requires psychological states or psychological capacities.

The conjunction of (A) and (B) is likely to result in a mislocation of the time when people begin to exist and cease to exist. This is particularly obvious in the case of beginnings. Each of us existed not only at the time of his or her birth but at some time before birth, as a prenatal being. This plain fact, as I take it to be, cannot be reconciled with the conjunction of (A) and (B), since—as Tooley's arguments suggest—no prenatal being has the psychological capacity that is required to qualify as a person. If we mean to adopt a realistic view as to when we first exist, I believe we do well to reject (A). Each of us once existed as something that was not a person—as an unborn fetus. This means that "person" does not locate the form of people. To specify an individual's Aristotelian form is to specify at least part of what it is to *be* this individual. Since I once existed as a nonperson, it cannot be true that being a person is part of what it is to be me.

I believe the same point emerges when we turn away from beginnings and consider endings. Most of us dread the prospect of dying. Why is death regarded as a bad thing—an evil? It might be said that death is a bad thing because it marks the time when we cease to exist, cease to be part of the world. In an article entitled "Death," the American philosopher Thomas Nagel says:

> It is true that both the time before a man's birth and the time after his death are times when he does not exist. But the time after his death is time of which his death deprives him. It is time in which, had he not died then, he would have been alive.[18]

Death is a bad thing because it deprives us of good things—pleasant experiences such as conversations with friends and loved ones, the realization of goals, the exhilarating feeling of fresh mountain air and sea breezes. This seems to be plausible enough. However, it should be noted that this deprivation account of why death is bad is independent of the thesis that we perish when we die—that is, perish when our bodies cease to function electrically and chemically. I suspect that we do well to question this thesis. It may be true, as (B) suggests, that a dead "person" is not really a person at all. But unless we accept (A), it does not follow from this that we perish at the time of our biological death. If we can exist as nonpersons before birth, perhaps we also will exist—at least for a short time—as nonpersons after death. The corpse lying in the morgue may be my friend Ralph, even though the corpse does not qualify as a person. Ralph exists both before birth and after death as something other than a person. So "person" does not signify Ralph's Aristotelian form or essence.

My own view is that the term "Ralph" designates a certain human body. Throughout much but by no means all of its career, this body has the psychological capacities that qualify it as a genuine person. Neither the unborn fetus that exists shortly before Ralph's birth nor the corpse that exists after Ralph's death is a person. Nonetheless, the fetus and the corpse "both" are Ralph. Ralph's form or essence is specified by "human being" or "human body" but not by "person." Contrary to both Aristotle and Descartes, Ralph's mind is a material component of Ralph. Ralph's mind is Ralph's brain.

But does not Ralph's mind perish before Ralph's brain perishes? Obviously A cannot be *identical* with B if A perishes before B perishes. Since Ralph's mind perishes when Ralph ceases to have thoughts, desires, and consciousness, it seems that Ralph's brain but not Ralph's mind continues to exist in the morgue. Must it not then be a mistake to identify Ralph's mind and Ralph's brain?

Briefly stated, my reply to this is as follows: the object that is Ralph's mind (namely, Ralph's brain) continues to exist after it ceases to function psychologically and therefore after it ceases to be a *mind.* The things that are our minds can, and in the natural course of events frequently do, continue to exist for some time after they cease to be minds. It is true that a corpse does not have a mind. Nonetheless, one component of a corpse is something (a brain) that previously *was* a mind. Just as a bachelor can continue to exist after ceasing to be a bachelor, a mind can continue to exist after ceasing to be a mind. The brain of a corpse is a former mind. So in a sense our minds do not perish at the moment we die.

CHAPTER 8

Responsibility

To say that a person has an immaterial soul is not to say that if you examine him closely enough under an acute enough microscope you will find some very rarefied constituent which has eluded the power of ordinary microscopes. It is just a way of expressing the point within a traditional framework of thought that persons can—it is logically possible—continue when their bodies do not.

RICHARD SWINBURNE, IN *PERSONAL IDENTITY* (1984)[1]

Materialism is consistent with our intuitions concerning our special status as moral beings.

MICHAEL E. LEVIN, *METAPHYSICS AND THE MIND-BODY PROBLEM* (1979)[2]

8.1 Resurrection Revisited

Many people firmly believe in the possibility of some sort of after-life. There are variations on the story. Some people believe that they will exist in the future in some otherwordly place called "heaven" or "hell." But, of course, one might believe in an afterlife without believing in heaven or hell. One might believe that it is in theory possible that a supernatural being (God) will arrange things so that one exists *in this world* in, say, the twenty-fifth century. Is it not at least *possible*—not *true* but *possibly true*—that God will arrange things so that I attend a World Series game between the Yankees and the Dodgers in the twenty-fifth century, hundreds of years after my death in (as I anticipate it will be) the twenty-first century? Suppose that the answer is affirmative. We then have the ingredients for an impressive argument opposing the view that we are (identical with) our present bodies. If we employ the term "Ralph" to name the object that presently is my body, the argument has this form:

(1) If Carter = Ralph then *necessarily* Carter = Ralph.

(2) If *necessarily* Carter = Ralph then *necessarily* Carter permanently ceases to exist when Ralph permanently ceases to exist.

(3) If *necessarily* Carter permanently ceases to exist when Ralph permanently ceases to exist, then it is not *possible* that Carter will and Ralph will not exist in the twenty-fifth century.

(4) In fact, it is *possible* that Carter will and Ralph will not exist in the twenty-fifth century.

Therefore

(5) It is not true that Carter = Ralph.

I think that the first three premises of this argument are true. If, as many people firmly believe, the fourth premise is also true, then I grant that Ralph (my body) and I are not one. But (4) gives me pause. It is possible, I suppose, that someone attending a World Series game in the twenty-fifth century will have apparent memories of living in the twentieth century and doing many of the things that only I did in this period. Does *this* show that (4) is true? For reasons that surfaced in Chapter 7, I doubt that it does. The fact that some future person seems to remember doing things that only I previously did cannot be sufficient for judging that this person is me, since it might happen that two or even more future people seem to have such memories. And it is impossible for two (or more) future people both to be me.

Granted, this does not establish that (4) is false. Suppose, contrary to what I believe, that (4) were to turn out to be true. In that case (5) would be true as well. This would leave us with the question:

Carter = ?

It is no doubt true that I am a person. But what is a person if not a human body? It might be replied that a person is a composite entity made up of a body and a mind. This is redundant if minds are brains (since brains are parts of our bodies). But of course, if it is possible for our minds to exist at times when our (present) brains do not exist, our minds are *not* our brains. How are we to decide whether such a thing *is* possible?

8.2   An Argument from Responsibility

We might suspect that we cannot conclusively resolve the possibility question unless we first know whether our minds are our brains. But how are we to attain such knowledge? Some theorists believe that careful attention to the fact that we are morally responsible for our actions shows that our minds are not our brains. The first part of the argument proceeds as follows:

(1) Everything that is part of the material world works in a deterministic way.

(2) If our minds were our brains, then our minds would be part of the material world.

(3) Our minds do not work in a deterministic way.

Therefore

(4) If our minds were our brains, our minds would work in a deterministic way [from (1) and (2)].

(5) Our minds are not our brains [from (3) and (4)].

Obviously we cannot assess this without some grasp of what it means to say that something "works in a deterministic way." I'll have more to say about this in the chapter that follows. For now, let us assume that things that work in a deterministic way are such that their behavior can in theory be predicted with scientific certainty.[3] Should we then accept the present argument? In particular, do we have any reason to judge that premise (3) is true?

The second part of the argument is a defense of (3):

(6) If our minds worked in a deterministic way, then we would not have free will.

(7) If we did not have free will, then we would not be responsible for our actions.

(8) But we are responsible for our actions.

Therefore

(9) = (3) Our minds do not work in a deterministic way.

On occasion we *blame* people and even *punish* them for what they do. Ascription of blame and infliction of punishment presuppose that a person bears responsibility for his or her actions. In turn, the plausible assumption that people are responsible, at least in many cases, for their actions implies that those who act have genuine *alternatives* to acting as they do. A person is hardly blameworthy for acting in a certain way in circumstances where he or she simply could not act in any other way. Is it really true that people have it within their power to do things they did not in fact do? As we shall see in Chapters 9 and 10, there are interesting arguments purporting to show that none of us *can* ever do anything other than that which we *do*. If these arguments are sound, it is hard to see how we can ever bear genuine responsibility for our acts. The fact that we undoubtedly *will* be held responsible for many of our actions does not cut any ice. It does not follow from the fact that someone is *held* responsible for an action that this person really *is* responsible for this action. Sadly, people are often held responsible for the performance of actions for which they bear no responsibility.

One way of attacking the argument in (1) through (9) is by denying that people ever bear responsibility for their actions. Most of us find this extremely counterintuitive. I will simply assume, for the time being, that in normal circumstances people *can* act in ways other than the ways they do act and that they generally (though not invariably) bear responsibility for their actions. These are immensely plausible assumptions. The question is: Can such assumptions be reconciled with a "materialist" analysis of what a person is? In particular, can such assumptions be reconciled with the claim that our minds are our brains? It is not hard to see how a negative answer to such questions might appear justified. Descartes suggests that the human body be "regarded as a machine which having been made by the hands of God, is incomparably better arranged, and possesses in itself movements which are much more admirable, than any of those which can be invented by man."[4] Machines do not have free will. If our minds were our brains, our minds would be machines (brains) embedded in other machines (our bodies)—in which case we would not have free will. But we *do* have free will. So it simply cannot be true that our minds are our brains.

8.3   A Question of Consistency

I have reservations about such arguments. In particular, I am not convinced that the argument in (1) through (9) has consistent premises. Let me explain.

Suppose that our minds are some sort of immaterial substances that somehow produce results in our bodies. For example, suppose that when I decide to stand up and get a drink of water it happens that the immaterial substance that is my mind causes my body to move in the direction of the tap in the kitchen. If premise (3) is true, then it could not be scientifically predicted that I (my mind) would make the decision to get the water. Since this decision caused the movement of my body, it seems that it could not be scientifically predicted that my body would move toward the kitchen. This means that my *body* does not work in a deterministic way. Since my body clearly is part of the material world, premise (1) is false. If it is true that our minds do not work deterministically, then it must be false that everything that is part of the material world works in a deterministic way.

Of course this argument falls apart if our minds do not produce results in our bodies. If that is so (if minds do not cause bodies to move), then the alleged unpredictability of the mind does not carry over to the body. Conceivably it then might be true both that our bodies do and that our minds do not work in deterministic ways.

However this raises a new, I think *fatal* problem. Premises (1) and (3) can both be true only if it is not true that our minds produce movements in our bodies. But it is very hard to see how (8) can be true if indeed our minds do not produce bodily movements. Suppose that my mind does not produce the movement of my finger when my finger pulls the trigger of the gun (firing the gun and killing someone). Can I then be responsible for the trigger pulling and its effects? I doubt it. More generally, I fail to see how (8) can be true if, indeed, our minds are causally isolated from our bodies. (On the other hand, if our minds are not causally isolated from our bodies, I do not see how premise (3) and premise (1) can be reconciled.)

We might believe that the material world is *closed* in the sense that everything that happens in it can in theory be explained in terms of material causes. If this is right, the mind is a spiritual substance only if the mind is causally isolated from what happens in the material world. But such isolation simply cannot be reconciled with the commonsense view that people are morally and legally responsible for their actions. How can a gunman be held responsible for shooting someone if, indeed, the gunman's decision to pull the trigger does not produce the movement of the trigger finger?

The likely reply to this is that the material world is not closed. Why should we accept this? Clearly there are physiological (physical) explanations of why the gunman's finger tightens on the trigger. Perhaps chemical and electrical events in the gunman's brain trigger the movement of the trigger finger. If so, I think we should conclude not that the gunman's mind plays no causal role in the movement of the finger but that the gunman's decision to pull the trigger is in fact a physiological event in the gunman's brain. If decisions are not determined in the sense that decisions are not in theory predictable with certainty, it is simply false that everything that happens in the material world happens in a deterministic way.

8.4 Human Chauvinism

Some people argue as follows:

(1) If our minds were our brains, then we (people) would be capable of acting freely if and only if *machines* are capable of acting freely.

(2) Machines are not capable of acting freely.

(3) We are capable of acting freely.

Therefore

(4) Our minds are not our brains.

One suspects that such arguments rest upon the tacit premise that people turn out to *be* machines unless people have an immaterial component called a "mind." We might wonder about this. If everything that a dog or cat does can be explained in physical terms, without postulating the existence of any immaterial substance that is a dog or cat component, does it follow that dogs and cats are machines? If we answer affirmatively, then it is not clear, to say the least, that (2) is true. Surely dogs and cats are *psychological* beings. As such, dogs and cats not only experience sensations and have desires but also make decisions. Does not the capacity for decision making entitle us to say that such individuals have "free will"? And if so, is it not perfectly conceivable that machines have free will?

It might be said that a machine is, properly speaking, something that is an artifact—roughly, something made in a factory. If so, dogs and cats are not machines after all. But we may agree that such nonmachines have minds and also doubt that any immaterial substance feels canine and feline pain and makes canine and feline decisions. I see no reason why we should not take the same approach when it comes to people. Why should a person not be regarded as a decision-making nonmachine whose mind is its brain? Until we have a satisfactory answer to such questions, premise (1) looks shaky at best. If canines can act freely even though canine minds are canine brains, why cannot humans act freely even though or if human minds are human brains? The fact that toasters and air conditioners do not act freely has little if any bearing upon questions pertaining to the nature of our minds.

In short, I see no good reason to deny that individuals having only material components or parts have thoughts and preferences and make decisions and choices. What about computers? Cannot a chess-playing computer decide to move a bishop from one place on the board to another? We do not normally think of computers as having "souls"—immaterial components that have the capacity to think. Nonetheless, it certainly seems that computers make decisions.

According to some theorists, "Computers are not free; ergo, if we are computers, or like them, we are not free either."[5] If computers in theory cannot be *free,* then computers cannot be *responsible* (blameworthy, praiseworthy) for their actions. What are the implications of this? There is perhaps a temptation to conclude that computers do not or cannot have *minds.* It seems to me that we do well to resist this temptation. Some mentally impaired human beings fail to be responsible for their actions. Such unfortunate individuals have sensations, desires, hopes, and fears—and so have minds—even though they do not bear responsibility for their actions. This shows that it does not follow from the claim that an individual has a mind that this individual is responsible for his or her actions. So even if it is true that computers cannot bear responsibility for their actions, we cannot conclude that computers do not have minds.

What assurance do we have that computers are not—or at any rate, could not be—free? One hears it said that computers only do things they are *programmed* to do. Perhaps in this respect computers are not different from us:

All of us were "manufactured" in placentas, "programmed" by a generous endowment of instinct, and are periodically "reprogrammed" by experience.[6]

Many people resist this suggestion. Such people argue that human decisions and actions simply cannot be predicted with certainty; on this basis, they may conclude that human behavior is not programmed. I think this is another bad argument. Even if it is true that our behavior is not scientifically predictable, it does not follow that there is no sense in which our behavior is "programmed" by our genetic code and the way we are conditioned. From the fact that we cannot predict what moves an advanced chess-playing computer will make in a given situation, it does not follow that the computer is not programmed to make the moves it makes.

All this leaves us with many hard questions. Even if having a mind does not entail responsibility for one's actions, we might believe that bearing responsibility for one's actions entails having a mind. If this is right, and it can be shown that computers do not (or cannot) have minds, then we will have grounds for concluding that computers do not (cannot) bear responsibility for their actions.

Some people maintain that only human beings have minds. Such chauvinism can perhaps be traced to the convictions that (1) nonhumans generally (canines, felines, chess-playing computers) do not have immaterial substances as components and (2) minds are immaterial substances. As indicated earlier, I think we should accept (1) and reject (2). If, as I suspect, all human behavior can be explained in physical terms, assumption (2) has the corollary that our minds are causally isolated from our behavior—a result that cannot be reconciled with the (apparent) fact that we (humans) are responsible for our actions.[7]

8.5   Is the Mind a Substance?

Of course this argument opposing (2) collapses in the event that it merely appears that (normal) humans are responsible for their actions. We will examine this responsibility assumption more closely in the two chapters that follow. For now I will simply assume that normal humans are beings that bear responsibility for their actions.

Suppose that I intentionally and, indeed, maliciously cause someone great pain and that you *blame* me for what I have done. Assuming that I bear responsibility for my action and also that I would not bear such responsibility if my mind were an immaterial substance, it follows that my mind is not an immaterial substance. But can we conclude from this that my mind is a *material* substance?

I think not. Conceivably our minds might turn out not to be *sub-stances* at all, in which case it would be false *both* that minds are material substances and that minds are immaterial substances. Perhaps it is true that there are minds but false that minds are substantial things.[8] David Hume (1711–1776), a Scottish philosopher, appears to take this view of things seriously. In a famous work entitled *A Treatise of Human Nature*, Hume writes:

> . . . we may observe, that what we call a *mind,* is nothing but a heap or collection of different perceptions, united together by certain relations, and suppos'd, tho' falsely, to be endowed with a perfect simplicity and identity.
>
> For my part, when I enter most intimately into what I call *myself,* I always stumble on some particular perception or other. . . . I never can catch myself at any time without a perception, and never can observe any thing but the perception. When my perceptions are removed for any time, as by sound sleep, so long am I insensible of *myself,* and may truly be said not to exist. And were all my perceptions removed by death . . . I should be entirely annihilated.[9]

When Hume speaks of "myself," perhaps he is referring to his mind.[10] If so, his position appears to be that a mind is neither a single material thing (for example, a brain) nor a monadic immaterial substance. When we attempt to examine our minds, we come across a *collection*—if you will, a *bundle*—of unsubstantial *psychological states:* ideas, thoughts, emotions, memories, and sensations. We do not encounter any substantial entity when we focus attention upon our mind (self). The Humean mind, or "soul," is properly compared not to a monadic substance but rather to a "republic or commonwealth."[11] We are not dealing with a single thing—and so not with a substantial thing—but rather with a collection or bundle of things.

Some contemporary theorists sympathize with Hume's proposed parallel between the self, or the mind, and commonwealths. Thus the Oxford philosopher Derek Parfit says that "[a] person is like a nation."[12] Let us pursue this. How is a person like a nation?

Suppose that I propose to show a child France. We fly across the Atlantic, depart from our plane, rent a car, and spend several weeks traveling from one place to another. At the conclusion of our trip, I notice that my companion is disheartened. Inquiry reveals that the child feels cheated. "I saw many things—many buildings, people, mountains, rivers, vineyards—but I never got to see the nation of France," she bitterly complains.[13] How should I reply to this? Perhaps the best that can be done is this: It is true that my companion did not encounter a *single* entity that can itself properly be identified with France—the nation. But it does not follow from this that my companion was cheated, that she did not get to see France. France is simply not a single thing. France is, rather, a collection of many things—many people, buildings, rivers, and so on. Since my companion saw many of the things that are in the collection of things that make up France, she saw a good deal of France. She was not cheated.

Perhaps in this respect a self or mind is like a nation. As I set out to examine my self, I encounter various thoughts, ideas, moods, and memories. I might feel cheated. Where is this elusive thing that is my mind or my self, I ask. Hume would argue that the question rests upon the mistaken premise that a mind is a *single* thing. It is true that I did not encounter a single thing that can correctly be called my self. But I should not feel cheated. For my self is not a single thing. It is, rather, a collection of many things—many ideas, moods, experiences, and memories. Much as a child might conclude from the fact that she does not see a single thing called "France" that France is an *invisible* entity, a philosopher might conclude from the fact that no single thing he or she observes is a mind that minds are invisible things. Hume rejects this reasoning. The mind or self is not a single invisible entity. Rather, it is a collection of many things, each of which can, in some introspective sense, be observed.[14]

8.6   Chisholm's Objection

Some people think that Hume is wrong about this. Among them is Roderick M. Chisholm, who writes:

> Our idea of "a mind" (if by "a mind" we mean, as Hume usually does, a person or a self) is not an idea only of "particular perceptions." It is not the idea of the perception of love or hate and of heat or cold. It is an idea of that which loves or hates, and of that which feels cold or warm (and, of course, of much more besides). That is to say, it is an idea of an x such that x loves or x hates and such that x feels cold and x feels warm, and so forth.[15]

Obviously there cannot be a smile or a frown unless there is a subject that smiles or frowns. Chisholm's objection to Hume's theory of the mind rests upon the same point: there cannot be love, hate, pleasure, or pain unless there is a subject who loves, hates, or feels pleasure or pain. The subject cannot be identified with any collection of experiences or feelings, since experiences and feelings require a subject—someone who has the experiences or feelings in question. Hume tells us that the self is no more than a collection of things. Chisholm replies that the things in the collection cannot exist unless there is first a self to serve as their subject. Since love, hate, hunger, fear, and "perceptions" generally *presuppose* a subject, we cannot identify the mind—that which is the subject—with any collection of experiences.

But perhaps there is a reply to this. Perhaps when Hume speaks of the mind or the self he means to refer not to a *whole* person but to what some theorists call a proper part of a person.[16] If so, Hume might argue that a person consists of a *body* and a *mind*. He might proceed to argue that the mind is no more than a collection of experiences—love, hate, hunger, and so on—had by the body. This answers Chisholm, since it allows for the fact that experiences presuppose a subject. (Your body is the subject of the various experiences that collectively make up your mind.) And it allows Hume to adopt the view that a person's mind is a collection of experiences.

We may have misgivings about this, too. Consider the fact that the collection of experiences that would on Hume's view be said to be the mind of Morning Alice—the person who climbs out of a certain bed in the morning—is generally if not invariably quite different from the collection of experiences that allegedly is the mind of Evening Alice, the (same) person who climbs into the same bed in the evening. If we identify Alice's mind with the former collection of experiences, then we cannot *also* identify Alice's mind with the latter collections of experiences. Let the term A1 name the collection of experiences Morning Alice has and term A2 name the collection of experiences Evening Alice has. If we say both that:

(1) Alice's mind = (is identical with) A1

and

(2) A2 = (is identical with) Alice's mind

then we will be forced to conclude that:

(3) A1 = (is identical with) A2

But statement (3) is simply not true. Since collection A2 includes some or many perceptions and experiences that are not part of collection A1, we cannot say that A1 and A2 are the same collection of perceptions and experiences. (The indiscernibility of identity principle, which was discussed in section 6.6, rules out the proposal that A2 can be identified with A1.) Since (3) is false, we cannot accept both statement (1) and statement (2). Since (1) and (2) appear to stand or fall together, it appears that we have reason to reject *both* statements. Alice's mind cannot be identified either with the collection of experiences Alice has in the morning or with the collection of experiences Alice has in the evening.

Many different collections of experiences are present at different times in a person's life. Should we say that a person has different minds at different times? Can it plausibly be said that Alice has *one self* in the morning and yet *another self* in the evening? Somehow this sounds implausible. Alice may have one husband in the morning and another husband in the evening. But it is not clear that things work the same way when we turn from husbands to selves. How can Alice have (be) one self in the morning and still another self in the evening?

Conceivably it might be argued that this is perfectly possible. Suppose that Alice is happy in the morning and sad in the evening. Alice's morning self is happy, Alice's evening self is sad. Since a happy thing is different from a sad thing, Alice's morning self is different from Alice's evening self. Since different things are not the same, it might be concluded that it makes perfect sense to judge that Alice's evening self is not the same as Alice's morning self.

8.7   The Responsibility Objection

It is hard to see how your evening self could be responsible for the misdeeds of your morning self, if indeed two different selves are at issue. If Evening Alice and Morning Alice are distinct selves, why blame Evening Alice for Morning Alice's kicking of the cat? The very fact that we *do* hold Evening Alice responsible for Morning Alice's actions suggests that it is hard to take seriously the proposal that we wake up in the morning with one mind or self and go to bed in the evening with still another mind or self. Surely I have the same mind in the morning and in the evening. A person does not have a different mind every time she changes from being glad to being sad. (To say that one's mind is in a qualitatively different state in the morning and in the evening does not imply that one has numerically different minds in the morning and in the evening. Similarly, to say that the bicycle I have in the morning is qualitatively different from the bicycle I have in the evening does not imply that I have one bicycle in the morning and another, numerically different bicycle in the evening.) It is, in brief, hard to take seriously the Humean proposal that we feign the identity of the mind.

But there are interesting complications. Consider a football game that lasts for an hour. We observe the entire game. In some sense, we *are* seeing the same game from one minute to the next. The events we observe one minute are *parts* of the game, as are the events we observe the *next* minute. The game itself is only *partly present* at any given moment, since some (many) of its segments or parts are not taking place at any given moment. At no given moment is the game *all present.* At no given moment does the game wholly or entirely exist. (What we see at any particular moment are events that constitute a small segment or part of the game.) The game is a *process* or *event*; therefore it is something that can be divided into *temporal segments* or temporal parts. Perhaps things work the same way when we turn from games (storms, love affairs, wars) to trees, rivers, and even people. Perhaps a person's mind has a temporal dimension in the sense that it can be broken down into various temporal segments or temporal parts. The collection of experiences associated with Alice's body in the morning is one part of Alice's mind; the collection of experiences associated with this same body in the evening is still another part of Alice's mind. Different segments or parts of Alice's mind exist at different times during Alice's life. No part of Alice's mind is a substantial thing. Each such part is, as Hume's comments might suggest, a collection of experiences. Morning Alice and Evening Alice are two things—two collections of experiences—that are distinct (temporal) parts of the same self. Just as different collections of molecules, existing at different times, may be parts of the same river, different collections of experiences may turn out to be parts of the same process/self.

Should we accept this? As it happens, there is an impressive argument opposing the view that the self is a process. Once again the objection turns upon the fact that people are often legally and morally *responsible* for actions performed in the past.

Alice robs a bank in 1970 and is not caught until 1980. The evidence against Alice is conclusive, and the judge "throws the book" at her—finding Alice guilty and sentencing her to twenty-five years in prison. Here Alice is (as we may suppose) justly *punished* for her misdeed. Punishment presupposes responsibility for past actions. The question is: Can defenders of the process analysis of the self allow that people bear responsibility for past actions? Critics argue that they cannot. Thus D. H. Mellor argues that no process analysis of people can be reconciled with the plain fact that people bear responsibility for things they have done. "Nothing and no one can be held responsible for an earlier action unless he, she or it is identical with whoever or whatever did that earlier action."[17] Responsibility requires

> . . . the self-same entity to be wholly present both when the deed was done and later when being held accountable for it—a condition satisfiable by things, but not by events. Because they have temporal parts, extended events . . . are never wholly present. In particular, whatever temporal parts of them caused the deed in question will never be the same as the parts which might later be brought to court for it. In short, social and psychological events can never be held morally or legally responsible for anything because they always have temporal alibis.

You might react to this with a shrug. Of course, you might say, *events* cannot be held responsible in any moral or legal sense. What bearing does this platitude have on the task of analyzing what a self is? The answer is that this platitude does not bode well for any process analysis of the self—any analysis that says that a self is a temporally extended thing having different temporal segments. How can we *blame* the 1980-segment of Alice for things done by the 1970-segment of Alice? In short, Mellor's responsibility objection comes down to this:

(1) If people are temporal processes (events), then people are never responsible for things they did earlier.

(2) It is not true that people are never responsible for things they did earlier.

Therefore

(3) It is not true that people are temporal processes.

As Mellor argues, the process analysis offers everyone a perfect "temporal alibi" for any charge of misconduct. My present self did not steal the money, only one of my previous selves. Why punish my present self for something one of my previous selves did? We may well judge that this line of defense is not very plausible. Since people are responsible for their previous actions—actions performed by their "previous selves"—we may suspect that our present selves are strictly identical with (though in some ways qualitatively different from) our previous selves. In short, the fact that we *are* responsible for previous actions suggests that the process analysis of the self deserves to be regarded with skepticism.

It seems we have reason to allow that people are not processes extended through time but rather, as Aristotelians argue, enduring or persisting substances that are (unlike events) "all present" at any moment at which they exist. More cautiously, it seems that the process analysis of the self must be rejected if indeed people bear responsibility for their actions. Common sense assures us that this responsibility assumption is true. But as we shall soon see, this assumption does not go unchallenged.

CHAPTER 9

Causal Determinism

Determinism is quite simply the thesis that the past *determines* a unique future.

PETER VAN INWAGEN, AN ESSAY ON FREE WILL (1984)[1]

But why do we want so much to hold others responsible? Could it be a streak of sheer vindictiveness or vengefulness in us, rationalized and made presentable in civilized company by a gloss of moral doctrine?

DANIEL C. DENNETT, ELBOW ROOM (1984)[2]

9.1 The Asymmetry of "Openness"

It is natural to think that the past and the future are different in the respect that the past is *closed* whereas the future is *open*. The idea behind talk of a "closed" past and an "open" future is not hard to grasp. To say that the past is closed is to say that we have no way of undoing what is done. From the vantage point of the present, events that have occurred are *necessary*. We simply lack the power to undo what is done—to *change* what has already happened. Intuitively the future is not like this at all. We regard the future as being "open" in the sense that we believe that we can, to some extent at least, *control* what does and does not happen in the future. Few people believe that the past is "open." What influence can we now have over events that have already happened?

We might say that event E is *necessary* at time T if and only if no one has at T the power to see to it that E does not occur. If we believe that the future is and the past is not "open," we then will accept:

(P) Where E is any event, if E has happened then E is now necessary.

and reject:

> (F) Where E is any event, if E will happen then E is now necessary.

Consider the event wherein John Kennedy is assassinated in Dallas. Since this event occurred many years ago, (P) tells us that this event is now necessary. At present no one can make it the case that Kennedy was not assassinated. This sounds right. Assuming that (P) is true, things work the same way regardless of which past event, however momentous or insignificant, we consider. If we were to accept thesis (F)—were to deny that the future is open—we would be committed to judging that any event that will happen in the future is presently such that it is necessary; that is, we would hold that no one presently has the power to see to it that this event does not occur. (F) is not intuitively plausible. Suppose that I plan to go to a concert tomorrow. If (F) were true, then no one would now have the power to see to it that I do not go to a concert tomorrow. But it seems that I do now have it within my power to see to it that I do not attend a concert tomorrow. I may simply decide not to go to the concert. Or, more radically, I may decide to end my life today—a decision that would result in my not attending the concert tomorrow. In light of such examples, it certainly *seems* that thesis (F) is false. Where "openness" is concerned, it seems that the past and the future are not symmetrical. As David Lewis says, "We tend to regard the future as a multitude of alternative possibilities. . . . whereas we regard the past as a unique, settled, immutable actuality."[3]

9.2   Law-governed Events

Rather surprisingly, there are interesting arguments in support of thesis (F). Common sense tells us that every event is caused by some prior event or events. Assuming that Davidson is correct in judging that causation involves lawlike regularities, it seems that every event—everything that happens—happens according to laws. If that is so, everything that happens at present is such that it could, in theory, have been predicted with certainty by someone who knew enough about the laws that govern the world and the past. But if things work this way when we consider the past and the present, it seems things work the same way when we consider the present and the future. Someone who knew enough about the present, and the laws that govern the world, could predict with absolute certainty what will happen a moment from now. This suggests that events in the future, events that will shortly occur, *cannot fail to happen.* And if future events cannot fail to happen, it seems we do not at present have it within our power to see to it that such events do not take place. Future events turn out to be no less necessary than past events.

Note that *civil* laws are not at issue here. Obviously it is not true that every event that takes place is governed by civil laws such as "Stop at red lights." Civil laws are made by groups of people. The laws of thermodynamics and the law of gravity are not made by groups of people. (Such laws are *discovered* by people, not *made* by people.) We have a certain amount of control over what is and is not a civil law. We can make new civil laws and eliminate old ones. But we do not seem to have any control over *natural* or *physical* laws. The laws of thermodynamics appear to obtain necessarily in a way that "Stop at red lights" does not. We have it within our power to *change* this last law, but not the former laws.

But how exactly does this establish the truth of thesis (F)? Conceivably defenders of (F) might argue along these lines:

(1) Natural laws are necessary.

(2) Every event is governed by natural laws.

Therefore

(3) Every event is necessary.

However, this is a suspect argument. Consider the similar argument:

(1*) Rules of chess are man-made.

(2*) Every chess move is rule governed.

Therefore

(3*) Every chess move is man-made.

Rules that are "man-made" are made by people. In light of this, it is clear that (3*) does not follow from (1*) and (2*). Since there are computers that may play chess, (3*) is false. Since (1*) and (2*) are true, it is clear that the (second) argument is unsound. Since the first argument has the same form as the second, we may doubt that the first argument is sound as well. Defenders of a closed future will have to do better than this if they hope to make a convincing case for their position.

But it is not hard to anticipate arguments in behalf of a closed future. Imagine a doctor who receives an emergency call and finds, upon rushing to the scene, that his patient has suffered a massive heart attack. Suppose, too, that there is lawful regularity between events wherein people have such heart attacks and events wherein people die. In such circumstances the doctor can hardly have it within his power to *save* his patient. It seems that *no one* can save the doctor's patient, since no one—excluding, perhaps, a supernatural being—has the power either to change the past or to do things that violate physical laws. None of us can throw a snowball that travels faster than the speed of light. Similarly, the doctor cannot save a patient whose life cannot be saved.

Causes precede their effects. Given this fact, it follows that every event that presently occurs is such that it is caused by some event or events that occurred previously. Assuming that (P) is true, these previous events are presently necessary. We do not at present have it within our power to make it the case that events that have already taken place do not occur. If causation involves law-governed regularities, it may be argued that every present event is no less necessary than is the patient's death. We do not have the power to bring it about that present events do not occur, given the fact that we are incapable of changing either the physical laws that govern the world or events in the past.

If we are *determinists,* we will proceed to argue that every event that will occur in the future is in precisely the same boat. If we knew enough about the past and the present and about the physical laws that govern the way things work, we could in theory predict *with absolute certainty* the occurrence of every future event. Events whose occurrence can be predicted with perfect certainty cannot fail to occur. Since we do not have any control over events that cannot fail to occur, future events turn out to be "necessary" in the sense specified earlier. The future turns out to be closed and not open.

Of course events that are now in the past were once in the future. Determinists argue that each such event is not only necessary now but is such that it was necessary before it occurred. Every event is causally determined by prior events, which themselves are causally determined by still earlier events. Causation is a transitive relation in the sense that if event E_1 causes E_2 and E_2 subsequently causes E_3, then E_1 causes E_3. Assuming that causation requires lawlike regularities, lawlike regularities obtain between present events and events that occur in the distant past as surely as they obtain between present events and events that will occur in the future. To be a *determinist* is to hold that we live in a world in which every event—past, present, and future—is causally determined and so necessary.

9.3   Two Versions of Determinism

There are many potential arguments opposing determinism. One is phenomenological. Certainly we *feel*, at least in normal circumstances, that we have control over some future events. Suppose that I plan to attend a certain concert tomorrow night. At present it seems that it is "up to me" whether I go or not. It *appears* to me that I have the power to bring it about that I stay away from the concert tomorrow—even though, by hypothesis, I in fact *will* go. Does this not show that some future events are not necessary?

Determinists deny that it does. Baron Holbach observes that "partisans of the system of free will appear ever to have confounded constraint with necessity."

> Man believes he acts as a free agent, every time he does not see anything that places obstacles to his actions; he does not perceive that the motive which causes him to will, is always necessary and independent of himself.[4]

Holbach's point is the following. There are no external *constraints* that prevent me from attending the concert. Nor is it true that a strong wind or a team of strong men will *force* me to attend. Nonetheless, despite the apparent absence of such compelling forces, Holbach would deny that it is possible for me not to attend the concert. The (future) event wherein I attend the concert is caused by my (future) *decision* to attend, which, in turn, is caused by events that are themselves caused by (past) events over which I have no control. In Holbach's view, the event that consists of my attending the concert is in precisely the same boat as is the event wherein the doctor's patient dies. Much as the doctor cannot *save* the patient, given what has happened in the past, I cannot *decide* to stay home tomorrow, given the events of the past.

Rather surprisingly, not all determinists would agree with Holbach's apparent rejection of the idea that on occasion people act *freely*. If determinism is true, every event—and so every action we perform and every decision we make—is made inevitable by lawful regularities and events in the past. Some theorists deny that it follows from this that we never act freely. Locke says:

> . . . so far as a man has power to think or not to think, to move or not to move, according to the preference or direction of his own mind, so far is a man *free*.

And again:

> A tennis ball, whether in motion by the stroke of a racket, or lying still at rest, is not by anyone taken to be a free agent. If we inquire into the reason, we shall find it is because we conceive not a tennis ball to think, and consequently not to have any volition, or *preference* of motion to rest, or vice versa. . . .[5]

It is not hard to anticipate what Locke would say concerning the possibility of computers that act freely. If—as some theorists argue[6]—computers can only simulate thought, computers cannot have *preferences* and so cannot act in ways that accord or conflict with their preferences. Locke would conclude that computers cannot be said to act either freely or unfreely. An agent acts freely when and only when this agent acts in accordance with its preferences; it acts unfreely whenever it acts contrary to its preferences. Beings that have no preferences act neither freely nor unfreely. Whether or not it is possible for machines to have preferences, *people* clearly do. Locke would argue that any action that any person freely performs is causally determined—determined by this person's (all things considered) preference for acting as he or she does.

Whether a computer can have preferences and thoughts is an issue that I cannot pursue here. For present purposes the important thing is that some determinists—they are often called *soft determinists*—are prepared to argue that it does not follow from the fact that every event is causally determined by previous events that people do not act freely. Suppose that I am doing what I want to do—acting in accordance with my preferences—when I attend the concert. Here soft determinists are prepared to argue that it is true that I act freely when I attend the concert and true also that my attendance at the concert is causally determined.

9.4   Slote's "Selective" Necessity

We may have misgivings about soft determinism. How can I be acting freely when I attend the concert if it is indeed *necessary* that I attend the concert? Hard determinists (as they are called) such as Holbach will argue as follows: Consider the state of the world as it was at the beginning of this century. Let W designate this inclusive state of the world at this time and L designate the sum (conjunction) of all the physical laws that govern the universe. It is *necessary* that if W and L obtain, then I attend the concert tomorrow. Since W is necessary and L is necessary, it is also necessary that W and L obtain. From this it follows that it is *necessary* that I attend the concert tomorrow. In light of this fact, I cannot be acting freely when I attend the concert. The fact that I am doing what I want to do when I show up at the concert does not, contrary to Locke, sustain the (false) claim that I freely attend the concert.

This certainly *sounds* promising. But does the present argument really establish that it is necessary—and not merely true—that I attend the concert tomorrow? Where C represents the statement that I attend the concert tomorrow, the argument has this form:

(1) Necessarily (if W and L then C).

(2) Necessarily (W and L).

Therefore

(3) Necessarily C.

Does the conclusion follow from the premises? Here we need to ask what *sort* of necessity we are dealing with. Very roughly, a statement is said to be *logically* necessary whenever the truth of this statement is guaranteed solely by the principles or rules of logic. It is logically necessary that either it will snow at the equator tomorrow or it will not. We do not need to know anything at all about weather patterns or the locations of low-pressure systems to know that *this* is so. The truth of this entirely trivial statement is assured by logic alone. Note that it is not logically necessary that I attend the concert tomorrow (though it *is* logically necessary that I either will attend or will not). Since (3) is false when interpreted in terms of logical necessity, the argument must either be invalid—which means that the conclusion does not follow from the premises—or have a false premise. In neither case is the argument sound.

The principles of logic do not, by themselves, guarantee the truth either of W or of L. The physical laws of thermodynamics, which are contained in L, are not guaranteed solely by rules of formal logic. Since these physical laws are constituents of W, the set of all the physical laws that govern the universe, W is not "logically true" or logically necessary. This means that premise (2) is false when interpreted in terms of logical necessity.

If the argument in (1) through (3) is to get off the ground, it must be interpreted in terms of some other sort of necessity. Perhaps hard determinists do better simply to observe that things (events, states) that are *unavoidable* are necessary. Since no decision we presently make can have the least influence on W, the state of the world as it was at the beginning of this century, it seems that W is presently unavoidable. For similar reasons, L seems unavoidable. (None of us can do anything to change or alter the physical laws that govern the world.) Premise (2) appears true on our present interpretation of "necessarily." Assuming, as all determinists hold, that lawful regularities hold between causes and their effects, premise (1) also appears true.

However, on the "unavoidability" analysis of necessity, it is not clear that conclusion (3) follows from (1) and (2). In a bold paper entitled "Selective Necessity and the Free-Will Problem," Michael Slote challenges this inference. If Slote is right, we can consistently grant that (1) and (2) are true and still deny that (3) is true. Slote says in one place:

> Certain past events will be necessary in the relevant sense (necessary in relation to the right sort of factor) and certain laws leading from them to an agent's later actions also will be necessary; but it will not follow that those actions are themselves necessary at some later time when the agent is considering whether to perform them. Of course, those actions will be *determined by* and presumably *predictable in terms of* factors prior to the agent's desires and abilities. But those earlier factors nonetheless bring such actions about only by means of (causal chains involving) later desires. . . . And what I have been claiming is that it is precisely this further aspect of the matter which is crucial to whether a given act is avoidable.[7]

Slote's position is very subtle. If I understand him, he would argue that the event wherein I go to the concert tomorrow is presently avoidable (for me) and so not necessary. Should I decide not to attend the concert, then I will not attend and C will turn out to be false. In this respect, C differs radically from W and L. No decision I can make will make either W or L false. Both W and L are unavoidable and so necessary. Slote denies that it follows from this that C is necessary. From my present standpoint, C is avoidable and so is not necessary. Unlike either W or L, C will turn out to be false if I make a certain decision.

Slote does not deny that every event is causally determined. On his view, the fact that an event is causally determined does not guarantee that it is *necessary*. He maintains that ". . . the ordinary notions of avoidability, inevitability, and the like involve the idea of being determined in a particular sort of way." In other words, an event is inevitable or necessary if it is causally determined by a series of events that involve no decisions or choices on the part of any agent. But things work differently when we consider events that are causally determined by a series of prior events that includes the making of a decision. The event that was the resignation of Richard M. Nixon as president is in this last category. Anyone who knew W and L could in theory predict with certainty that Nixon would resign when he did. Slote would deny that it follows from this that Nixon's resignation was inevitable or necessary. The resignation would not have occurred had Nixon not decided to resign. (Of course an impeachment rather than a resignation might well have occurred had things happened this way.) In light of this, Slote argues that the resignation event was not—from Nixon's standpoint—unavoidable. We could construct an argument such as the one above having the conclusion that it was necessary that Nixon resigned. The argument would be valid but would have false premises if it concerned logical necessity. It would have true premises but a false conclusion if it concerned the necessity of unavoidability. In neither case does it turn out that the argument is sound.

9.5   Fagan's Choice

Soft determinists will emphasize that many actions are caused by decisions we make. Following Slote, we may judge that such actions are not necessary. But are actions that are not necessary in this sense *freely* performed? It might appear that I freely attend the concert tomorrow. After all, the event wherein I attend is caused by the prior event that is my making a decision to attend. The case would be entirely different were my attendance at the concert caused by a remarkable and mysterious wind that, despite all my efforts at resisting, blew me into the concert hall. In this last case my decisions play no role in the causal chain of events that produces my attendance at the concert. Here it might appear true that my attendance at the concert is necessary and that I do not freely attend.

Generalizing on this, a soft determinist might defend the following principle:

> Where P is any person and A is any action performed by P, P does A freely if and only if P's doing of A is avoidable in the sense that P would not do A if P decided not to do A.

It is not hard to see how this might be given a Lockean twist. Our decisions reflect our "all things considered" preferences. So actions that are caused by our decisions seem to be actions that conform to our "all things considered" preferences. We act freely when we do things we want to do, all things considered. The fact that all of our actions are causally determined does not conflict with the claim that many of our actions are freely performed. As Locke argues, *freedom* consists in "our being able to act, or not to act, according as we shall choose or will."[8]

The "all things considered" clause should not be overlooked. You are walking through a park at night when a gunman appears and seriously announces that you will lose your life unless you hand over your money. In normal circumstances you would not want to hand over your money to a stranger. However, in special circumstances you may, all things considered, want to do just this. You prefer handing over your money to losing your life and so decide to hand the money over. On Locke's view, it seems that you are acting freely when you give the gunman your money.

Is this right? In a brilliant work entitled *The Nichomachean Ethics,* Aristotle argued that actions that are performed under compulsion are not voluntary. Can an action fail to be voluntary and also be freely performed? We may doubt this. If we are right, we should reject the claim that you act freely when you give the gunman your money. Certainly you are acting under compulsion—and not acting voluntarily—when you hand over the money.

Whatever our assessment of the gunman case, we may on reflection have misgivings concerning the present analysis of what it is to act freely. Suppose that Fagan is a heroin addict who had been without a fix for several days and is suffering horribly. We put a needle before Fagan and announce "It is up to you—do as you please," whereupon Fagan immediately plunges the needle into his arm. Did Fagan act freely? The event wherein Fagan plunges the needle into his arm is caused by a decision Fagan makes. It appears that this event would not have occurred had Fagan made a different decision. Given this fact and the further fact that Fagan acts as he chooses—according to his preferences—Locke would conclude that Fagan is acting freely when he takes the fix. But we may question this assessment of the matter. Fagan's *decision* to take the fix is not something over which Fagan has any control. How can an action be freely performed when it issues from a decision over which the agent has no real control?

Heroin addicts, kleptomaniacs, and compulsive gamblers may have no "real choice" as to what they do even though they act according to their preferences. If causal determinism is true, all of us are in the same boat. Consider my decision to attend the concert. Determinists assure us that this event—the making of this decision—is caused by prior events over which I have no control and for which I cannot be responsible. Assuming that causation involves lawlike regularities, it seems I cannot make any decision other than the one I make. Of course I may *think* that it is "up to me" to decide what to do. But as Holbach and other hard determinists will be quick to argue, the fact that my decision is causally determined by prior events (which themselves are caused by prior events) over which I have no control indicates that I am mistaken about this. As in the Fagan case, it seems to be a corollary of determinism that none of us can really make decisions other than the decisions we in fact make. But how can actions that issue from such "decisions" be freely performed?

To his credit, Locke was aware of the problem. Locke argues at length that the question "Whether man's will be free or not" is "altogether improper."[9]

> This question carries the absurdity of it so manifestly in itself,
> that one might thereby sufficiently be convinced that liberty
> concerns not the will. For, to ask whether a man be at liberty
> to will either motion or rest, speaking or silence, which he
> pleases, is to ask whether a man can will what he wills, or be

pleased with what he is pleased with. . . . A question which, I think, needs no answer.[10]

Why does the question not need an answer? Locke's claim is apparently that the question rests upon a false assumption. An act is freely performed only on the condition that it conforms to the agent's will. If we ask whether acts of will—events wherein people make decisions—are freely performed, we are in effect asking whether an act of will conforms to the agent's will. I freely decide (will) to attend the concert only if I decide (will) so to decide. But if we can intelligibly ask whether the first decision is freely made, Locke would argue, then a similar question arises concerning the decision to make this decision: *this* decision—act of will—is freely made only if it conforms to a *third* decision to decide to decide to decide to attend the concert. The third decision is freely made only if it conforms to a fourth decision to make the third decision, and so on. We are, in short, left with a "regress" that Locke regards as an absurdity.[11] Locke concludes that the question "Is the will free?" is simply not a "proper" question. And we need not answer yes or no to questions that are improper.

However, I doubt that Locke is right about this. The supposed regress of acts of will (decisions) simply does not arise when we reject the idea that an action is free if and only if it conforms to the will of the agent. I doubt that you freely hand over your money to the gunman, even if it is true that the event wherein the money is handed over conforms to your "all things considered" will or preference. Since I reject Locke's analysis of acting freely, I think that we can ask whether the will is free without danger of encountering the absurdity that we must make decisions to make decisions to make decisions (and so on) before we can be said to act freely. I freely will, or decide, to attend the concert only on the condition that I have it within my power to decide not to attend the concert. Since it is hard to see how I can have such power if my decision to attend is causally determined by events that took place in the distant past, I remain skeptical of the soft determinist's claim that free will can be reconciled with determinism.

9.6   The Elusive Nature of Causation

Most of us firmly believe that in normal circumstances we act freely. But it may appear that this belief must be abandoned. How *can* we act freely if every event is determined by prior events? My inclination is to agree with *incompatibilists,* who argue that free will and determinism simply cannot be reconciled. We simply cannot have it both ways. If every event—and so every human action and every human decision—is indeed causally determined, I cannot see how we can ever act freely.

However, it should be noted that it is one thing to say that free will cannot be reconciled with determinism—the thesis that every event is determined by prior events—and quite another to say that free will cannot be reconciled with the idea that every event has a cause. Perhaps causation need not involve determinism. Conceivably it might turn out that it is true that every event is caused by some prior event or events and also false that every event is determined—such that it could in theory be predicted with absolute certainty given sufficient knowledge of prior events and the physical (natural) laws that govern the way things work. Perhaps causation need not work according to *physical laws,* contrary to Davidson (see section 3.6). If that is so, the fact, as I take it to be, that every event has a cause does not pose a challenge to the thesis that we act freely.[12] We can allow that free will and determinism are incompatible and also say that free will and universal causation are compatible.

If we take this line, we must obviously be prepared to analyze causation in a way that frees, so to speak, causation from determinism. Under what conditions does one event cause another event? Obviously temporal precedence is only part of the story. Causes occur before their effects, granted; but there is more than this to causation. (We can hardly conclude from the fact that the signing of the Declaration of Independence took place before the sinking of the *Titanic* that the former event caused the latter event.) We have some work to do if we propose that causation is not to be analyzed in terms of lawlike connections between events.

Under what conditions can we truly say that one event *causes* another? Suppose that event E1 first occurs, whereupon event E2 then occurs. Does this guarantee that E1 causes E2? It seems not. Jack sneezes in Boston, whereupon Jill—who knows nothing of Jack's sneeze—laughs in Dallas. In such a case we have no reason to believe that Jack's sneeze causes Jill's laughter. The fact that one event occurs shortly before another clearly offers no basis for concluding that the former causes the latter.

Can we do better? Hume offers an analysis of causation that may appear promising:

> We may define a CAUSE to be "An object precedent and contig-
> uous to another, and where all the objects resembling the for-
> mer are plac'd in like relations of precedency and contiguity to
> those objects, that resemble the latter."[13]

There are any number of questions concerning the proper interpretation of this passage. But if we substitute talk of "events" for talk
of "objects," perhaps Hume means something like this: event E1 is
the *cause* of event E2 if and only if:

(1) E1 shortly precedes E2.
(2) E1 and E2 are "contiguous" in the sense that they occur in
roughly the same place.
(3) Events resembling E1 are regularly followed by events resembling E2.

Jack's sneeze causes Jill's laughter only if these three conditions are
jointly satisfied. But it seems that neither condition (2) nor condition (3) is satisfied. So the Humean analysis of causation gives us the
correct result that the sneeze does not cause the laughter.

Things work differently when we consider Jack's depression.
The event wherein Jack learns he has failed a certain test appears
contiguous with the event wherein Jack becomes depressed. Moreover, events of the former sort are regularly followed by events of
the latter sort. Here a case can be made for saying that two events
satisfy conditions (1), (2), and (3) and so are related causally.

Note that Hume makes no mention of "necessity" or lawlike
connections when he defines causation. Indeed, Hume suggests that
necessity is not located in "external bodies" (things outside the
mind), observing that "necessity is something, that exists in the
mind, not in objects."[14] Hume does not say that *causation* exists only
in our minds. If common sense is clear about anything, it is that
causation is a pervasive feature of the "external" world—the world
as it is outside of our minds. Holding that necessity resides only *in*
the mind, Hume and his followers conclude that causation does not
require necessity. Since lawlike regularities between events involve
necessary connections between them, Humeans deny that causation
is properly analyzed in terms of lawlike regularities. Even if every
event is caused by prior events, it does not follow that every event
is *determined,* or made *necessary,* by previous events. We can accept
universal causation (that every event has a cause) without being

committed to universal determinism (that every event is necessary, given previous events).

It sounds promising. But on reflection we may suspect that causality cannot be analyzed in terms of regularity. For it seems that mere regularity of E1-like events and subsequent E2-like events does not offer any guarantee that the former events *cause* the latter. There is a perfect regularity between migration-of-bird events and waves-coming-onto-the-beach events. (Whenever events of the former sort occur, events of the latter sort take place.) However, we cannot conclude from *this* that the recent migration of geese from Canada *causes* the present arrival of waves on the beach at Malibu. Regularity is simply not sufficient for causation.

Of course migration-of-geese events are not "contiguous" with the events consisting of the arrival of the waves. But suppose that it happens that events wherein Jack laughs are regularly preceded by events wherein Jack smiles. Such Jack-smiling events and Jack-laughing events are contiguous—that is, they occur in the same place. But this offers no guarantee that the smiling events cause (produce, bring about) the laughing events. It might happen that the jokes Jill tells Jack cause both Jack's smiles and Jack's laughter (the laughter not being caused by the smiles).

There are other worries concerning the Humean analysis of causation. For one thing, the contiguity clause of the regularity analysis is itself questionable. Jack is in Boston when he calls Jill in Dallas and makes an offensive remark which angers Jill. Clearly the making-of-remark event causes the event wherein Jill becomes angry. Since the former event occurs in Boston and the latter event occurs in Dallas, *contiguity* can hardly be required for causation. Hume's regularity analysis must be revised to allow for the fact that causal relations connect sequences of events whose first and last members are not "contiguous" either spatially or temporally.

The case of the birds and waves might suggest that some regularities are "accidental" while others are not. We might believe that regularities that are *not* accidental play an important and indeed essential role in any proper analysis of causation. Such regularities might be said to be *lawlike,* not in the sense of being legislated by human beings but in the quite different sense of being guaranteed by "natural" physical laws that govern the world we inhabit. Defenders of this view argue, contrary to Hume, that necessity is essential to genuine causation. Since causation exists outside our minds, so does necessity.

But, as we saw earlier, it is hard to see how belief in free will is to be reconciled with the convictions (1) that causation involves lawlike regularities guaranteeing that effects are *necessary,* given their causes, and (2) that every event is caused by previous events. If we judge that it is a fact that people do act freely on occasion, we have reason to reject (1) and look for an analysis of causation that does not require lawlike necessities.

Perhaps we can do better than Hume did. One interesting proposal is that event E1 causes event E2 if and only if the occurrence of E1 serves, at least to some extent, to *explain* the occurrence of E2. Suppose that Jack makes a rude comment to Jill and that Jill subsequently breaks Jack's nose. Jill is in normal circumstances a calm and nonviolent person. Knowing this, Jill's friends may well ask what caused Jill to break Jack's nose. Upon learning of the nature of Jack's comment, Jill's friends find it understandable that she acted as she did. The event wherein Jack makes his nasty comment *explains* the event wherein Jill's fist breaks Jack's nose.

Perhaps this, or something close to this, is what is crucial to understanding the claim that it is the making of the comment that causes the breaking of the nose. Perhaps a cause is an event that serves to explain the occurrence of another event. (If more than one event is such that it serves to explain why something happens, then each of the events having such an explanatory role has claim to being a cause of what happens.) Note that we can accept this account of causation and also deny that this explanation always works in terms of strict deterministic laws. It may turn out to be true that Jack's comment explains the event that is Jill's hitting of Jack and it may prove false that the nose breaking was in theory inevitable or predictable with certainty (given the antecedent conditions and physical laws that govern the universe). If so, perhaps we can say that while the making of the comment *causes* Jill's hitting of Jack, it is nevertheless not true that the making of the comment *determines* Jill's hitting of Jack. Causation does not require determination. So even—as I believe—if free will and determination are incompatible, universal causation can perhaps be reconciled with free will.

No doubt such an appeal to "causation without necessitation" needs to be spelled out in greater detail. Certainly there are a number of potential objections to the proposal that causation can properly be analyzed in terms of explanatory role. There are a number of important and interesting questions that I cannot pursue further here. I can only record my conviction that, if it is true that causation requires determination, common sense cannot be right in telling us that we act freely.

CHAPTER 10

*F*ate

. . . anyone who really knew who Caesar was (in the sense of being able to distinguish him from all other possible individuals, however similar to Caesar they might be) would see that such a person had to cross the Rubicon.

BENSON MATES, *THE PHILOSOPHY OF LEIBNIZ* (1986)[1]

10.1   An Argument in Behalf of Fatalism

It is certainly true that what is done is done (what has happened has happened). It is equally true that what will be will be (what will happen will happen). Yet common sense tells us that the past differs significantly from the future. Somehow from the vantage point of the present the past seems to be beyond our control, fixed, or *necessary.* Common sense tells us that this is not true of the future. We regard the future, in most respects, as being "open" in the sense that there are alternative possibilities. To some extent, at least, it is up to us which of these various possibilities comes about or is realized.

Is common sense right in so regarding the situation? In the previous chapter we examined some arguments from causal determinism and saw how such arguments challenge (unsuccessfully, I think) this commonsense view of things. However, even if causation is left out of the picture, there are interesting arguments purporting to show that the future is fated and as such is no more "open" than the past.

Let us suppose it is true that I will drink a cup of tea ten minutes or so from now. You would have spoken truly had you said a moment ago that I will drink tea in about ten minutes. This poses a problem. Common sense tells us that I can bring it about that I will not drink tea at the indicated time. (I have it within my power not to drink tea at this time; I am not a tea junkie.) However there is an interesting argument opposing common sense that proceeds along these lines: Since the past is fixed, nothing I can do now or in the future can alter the fact that you spoke truly a moment ago when you said I will drink tea in ten minutes or so. Since my not drinking tea at the indicated time *would* bring it about that you did not speak truly when you said what you said, my not drinking tea at the indicated time is possible only if it is possible that I alter the past. Since I cannot alter the past, I cannot fail to drink tea at the indicated time. Thus the future event that is my drinking of the tea in ten minutes' time is something I cannot avoid. This event is necessary in precisely the way that events in the past are necessary. Indeed, this event is necessary precisely because the past is unalterable.

One can construct a similar argument in the case of *any* future event. Such "fatalist" arguments purport to show that the future is "closed" in precisely the way that the past is "closed." Since fatalism does not presuppose the truth of causal determinism, we cannot answer the fatalist by arguing against causal determinism.

Some theorists (Aristotle, for one) have replied to the fatalist by denying that statements about the future, at the time they are made, are either true or false. If Aristotle is right, you do not say something that is either true or false when you say that I will drink tea ten minutes from now. I think that this reply to the fatalist conflicts with common sense as surely as does the fatalist's thesis that the future is necessary (fated). Common sense tells us that you are entitled to say, witnessing my drinking of tea ten minutes from now, that you spoke truly when you said (a bit more than ten minutes ago) that I would drink tea at this time.

Nonetheless, I think there is a mistake in the fatalist's argument. The mistake lies with the assumption that it is never true that we have it within our power to alter the past.

In fact, I *can* bring it about that I do not drink tea throughout the rest of the day. Since you spoke truly when you said that I will drink tea shortly, I will not *exercise* this power. Still, I *do* have the power not to drink tea today. Since I have the power to do this, I have the power to do something that would, if done, make it the case that you spoke falsely a moment ago when you predicted that I would drink tea shortly. I can make your prediction false. Since your prediction is true, I can alter the past.

In taking this position, I am following the distinguished medieval philosopher William of Occam. Occam argues that we should distinguish between "hard" facts about the past, which cannot be altered, and "soft" ones, which *can* be altered. Since nothing I or anyone can do now or in the future can possibly change the fact that you made the prediction you made a moment ago, the fact that you made such a prediction is a hard fact about the past. Things are different when we consider the fact that your prediction is *true*. Since I have it within my power to make it the case that your prediction is *not* true, the fact that you made a true prediction a moment ago is a *soft* fact about the past. The fatalist's argument is unsound precisely because it rests upon the mistaken assumption that all facts about the past are hard facts. Or so I believe.

10.2   The Best of All Possible Worlds

But worries concerning fatalism are not so easily dismissed. Such worries may arise when we take seriously the proposal that the world we inhabit was created by a supernatural being, called "God," who somehow knows from the outset everything that will happen. Let us assume, for the moment, that God exists. (This assumption is critically considered in Chapter 11.) No doubt the conviction that God created the world will shape our conception of the world. At the same time, the creation conviction may shape our view of God. Conceivably we may learn things about God by examining God's creation. A theorist who views matters in this light might argue as follows:

(1) An individual who does not choose the best must lack either power (the power to choose something better), knowledge (the knowledge that something is better), or goodness.

(2) God did not choose the best when he created our world—the world we actually inhabit.

Therefore

(3) God must lack either power, knowledge, or goodness.

It is to Leibniz's credit that he anticipates this argument and formulates a reply. Leibniz accepts (1) and rejects (2) and (3). He agrees that the actual world God created contains imperfect parts, but he also argues that "an imperfection in the part may be required for the greater perfection of the whole.'' In short, Leibniz's position is that God is unsurpassably great when it comes to power, knowledge, and goodness. From this fact (as Leibniz takes it to be) together with (1), Leibniz arrives at the conclusion that the actual world we inhabit is the *best* world there possibly could be. God's unlimited power enables God to create all sorts of worlds—worlds that differ slightly or even radically from our world. But God's goodness and knowledge reflect the fact that no better world than ours is even theoretically possible.

Some of us have misgivings about this. A world in which injustice, violence, hatred, and disease are so abundant hardly appears to be the best world there possibly could be.[2] We would not judge of a human relationship that was characterized by violence and hatred that it was the best relationship there possibly could be. Why should things be any different when we turn from relationships to the world itself?

Voltaire wrote a famous work entitled *Candide*, in which he ridicules the proposal that our world is the best world that is possible. Voltaire's satiric work is filled with scenes in which Pangloss, an imaginary philosopher, is engaged in lengthy proclamations of the ''Everything is for the best'' theme, only to be interrupted by events of unspeakable horror and depravity. It is indeed hard to take Panglossian (or Leibnizian) optimism seriously in a world where children in Ethiopia are starving to death. Presumably God could have created a world in which such terrible events did not occur. Since such worlds appear to be improvements on the actual world we inhabit, it seems that God could—contrary to Leibniz—have created a better world.

10.3   The Free-Will Defense of Atheism

Defenders of God have an interesting reply to this. Very briefly stated, the reply is that worlds lacking evil (worlds in which, say, children are not napalmed) only *appear* to be improvements upon the actual world we inhabit. The thrust of the reply emerges when we consider an interesting little speech attributed to God by the logician Raymond M. Smullyan:

> . . . I created angels, and they have no free will. They are in actual sight of me and are so completely attracted by goodness

that they never have even the slightest temptation toward evil. They really have no choice in the matter.[3]

We might say that a world is *nice* if and only if no evil act is ever performed in it. Conceivably defenders of Leibniz will argue that nice worlds must be populated entirely by angelic individuals—beings who are so attracted by God's goodness that they simply cannot do evil. If this is right, even God could not create a nice world populated by individuals who have free will. It is better (defenders of Leibnizian optimism may argue) to have a world in which free agents sometimes do good and sometimes do evil than to have a world in which angelic robots, so to speak, always do good.

Such a defense of an unsurpassably perfect God rests squarely upon the assumption that those of us who inhabit the actual world are free agents who generally act freely. (It is often called "the free-will defense" of theism.) Interestingly enough, those who deny that there is an unsurpassably perfect God may base their case upon the same assumption (the assumption that we have free will).

One is an *atheist* if one believes that God is imaginary and not real. Conceivably an atheist might argue that we cannot consistently say both that God is real and that people have free will. Given the further premise that people *do* have free will (a premise defenders of God accept), it then follows that it is not true that God is real. Arguments having this form offer what might be called "free-will defenses of atheism."

Our atheist might begin as follows: if God is indeed real, then God knows, say, at the time of your birth everything that is true about you. God knows at this time that you will attend a certain primary school, do poorly in geography, marry a certain person, have a certain number of children, and so on. God knows at the time you are born everything that will happen to you throughout your entire life. More exactly, God knows this if God exists.

The atheist then proceeds (second step of the argument) to argue that such divine foreknowledge simply cannot be reconciled with the proposal that you ever act freely. If atheists are right about this, a metaphysical position that includes both belief in divine foreknowledge and belief in free will is simply *inconsistent.* We cannot have it both ways. Since there is—as atheists and theists agree—excellent reason to suppose that we do act freely, the atheist concludes that we must reject the proposal of divine foreknowledge.

Since the atheist holds that belief in God's reality commits us to belief in divine foreknowledge, the atheist concludes that we must reject belief in God's reality.

This is at any rate the *general* idea. Obviously the success of the free-will defense of atheism depends upon the thesis that divine foreknowledge and free will cannot be reconciled. Why should we accept this?

For the moment, let us forget about alleged *divine* foreknowledge. Instead let us focus upon *human* foreknowledge. Surely we do sometimes know certain things about the future. In particular, we sometimes know that a person will act in a certain way. Is such knowledge consistent with the claim that the person who is the object of our knowledge acts freely? If the question deserves an affirmative answer, we might suspect that the atheist must be mistaken in judging that divine foreknowledge cannot be reconciled with free will. However, atheists may argue that our present question does not deserve an affirmative answer. Let us consider one argument supporting this position.

Jill has been offered a lucrative and prestigious job in a certain law firm. But Jill will have to move to Chicago if she accepts the job. Jill's close friend Jack claims that he knows that Jill will refuse the job. Question: Can it be true both that Jack knows that Jill will refuse and that Jill acts freely when she subsequently does refuse the job?

It might be argued that both claims simply cannot be true. One argument supporting this view proceeds as follows:

(1) Necessarily, if Jacks knows that Jill will refuse, then Jill will refuse.

(2) Jack knows that Jill will refuse.

Therefore

(3) Necessarily, Jill will refuse.

(1) seems beyond question. If we suppose, for the sake of argument, that (2) is true, it is perhaps hard to see how (3) can be rejected. But if (3) is accepted, we are hardly in a position to say that Jill acts *freely* when she subsequently refuses the job. If it is *necessary* that Jill will refuse, then it is *not possible* that Jill will accept the job. And if this is not possible, Jill does not really have any genuine options when she refuses.

We might respond to this by rejecting premise (2). We might say that (2) is false precisely because Jill acts freely when she refuses the job. (If Jill acts freely, then she has different options. And if she has different options, no one can know in advance what she will do.) If we take this position, we are, in effect, granting that human foreknowledge and free will are incompatible. Atheists may well rejoice in this view of the situation. Precisely because people *do* act freely, atheists may conclude that there simply cannot be a God who has foreknowledge of what we will do.

There are, however, problems with the argument in (1) through (3). One problem emerges when we consider the fact that arguments with precisely the same structure are obviously unsound:

> **(1*)** Necessarily, if Jack is a bachelor, then Jack is not married.
>
> **(2*)** Jack is a bachelor.

Therefore

> **(3*)** Necessarily, Jack is not married.

The argument in (1*) through (3*) has precisely the same structure or form as does that in (1) through (3). But something clearly goes wrong with the bachelor argument. The plain fact of the matter is that the truth of (1*) and (2*) does not offer any guarantee at all that (3*) is true. (3*) tells us, in effect, that it is not possible for Jack to be a married man. No defender of the free-will defense of atheism (or theism) will be prepared to accept this. Clearly (3*) is false, even though (1*) and (2*) are both true. The point is of some importance, since it suggests that arguments having the form of (1*) through (3*) are not valid. (The conclusion simply does not follow from the premises.) Since the argument in (1) through (3) has precisely this form, it must then be judged invalid. Even if both the premises of this argument are true, we have no reason at all to conclude that it is true that Jill must necessarily refuse the job. The present case for judging that foreknowledge and free will cannot be reconciled thus collapses. Defenders of the free-will defense of atheism will have to do better than this if they hope to make their case plausible.

10.4 Leibniz's Analysis of Divine Foreknowledge

Jack may know that Jill will refuse the job because Jack knows a great many things about Jill's character, things that Jack has learned from years of acquaintance with Jill. But how can God possibly know, at the moment Jill is born, that Jill will refuse the job? God's knowledge cannot be based upon prior acquaintance with Jill, since Jill simply does not exist prior to this time. We are owed some account of how divine foreknowledge of an individual's career is possible even before this individual exists. Leibniz offers a very subtle and detailed analysis of such knowledge. Though I cannot do full justice to Leibniz's position here, perhaps I can bring the general idea into view. Let us begin by comparing the following two propositions:

(1) All U.S. senators are millionaires.
(2) All bachelors are unmarried.

Both statements are true. There is, however, an important difference between the two. We can somehow know that (2) is true without the empirical process of locating and then examining each and every individual who is a bachelor. Statements such as (2) are said to be *a priori truths* and not *empirical truths.* Such statements can somehow be known in a way that does not require examination of any individual person or thing. The situation is entirely different when we turn from (2) to (1). To know that (1) is true, we must really locate and then examine various individuals, namely, the various people who are senators. Accordingly, (1) appears to be an empirical truth and not an a priori truth. Although (1) and (2) are both true, it seems that they are true "in different ways." (1) is true because certain individuals have a certain quality or attribute (the quality of being a millionaire). If (2) were true for the same sort of reason, we would have to locate and then examine certain individuals—checking to see if they have the quality of being unmarried—to determine whether (2) is true. But in fact we do not have to proceed this way at all. Since we can know that (2) is true in some nonempirical (a priori) way, it seems that (2) is not true because certain individuals (bachelors) have a certain quality.

There is reason to think that, in Leibniz's view, "there is an a priori proof of every true proposition."[4] If this is right, Leibniz is not faced with any *special* problem when it comes to explaining how divine foreknowledge of a person's life is possible even before this person exists. In whatever way you and I know a priori (without examining any individual) that bachelors are unmarried, God knows a priori that Richard Nixon will resign as president. Ordinary people such as you and I can know things a priori. Divine foreknowledge of what a person's life holds in store is, though much more extensive than our knowledge, knowledge of the same sort.

Clearly we need a plausible account of how things can be known in an a priori manner. Before saying something about this, however, I should call attention to the fact that while an atheist may allow that certain human foreknowledge is consistent with human free will, he or she may also *deny* that *divine* foreknowledge of the Leibnizian sort is consistent with human free will. Let me outline the basis for this denial.

So-called a priori truths have traditionally been held to be *necessary* in the sense that there is simply no real possibility that such a proposition can be falsified.[5] This seems immensely plausible when we consider the statement "All bachelors are unmarried." Being unmarried is part of what it is for someone to *be* a bachelor. In light of this, there does not appear to be any real possibility that any individual qualifies as a bachelor who is not unmarried. It is precisely *because* there is no such possibility that we can be guaranteed in advance, before we have directly examined any individual or any individuals, that it is true that all bachelors are unmarried. All of this may cause us to doubt that divine foreknowledge is compatible with free will. The argument for incompatibility, briefly stated, goes as follows:

(1) If God has foreknowledge before Jill is born of the proposition that Jill will refuse the job, then the proposition that Jill will refuse the job must be an a priori (and not an empirical) truth.

(2) If the proposition that Jill will refuse the job is an a priori truth, then this proposition is a *necessary* truth (since all a priori truths are necessary truths).

(3) If the proposition that Jill will refuse the job is a necessary truth, then there is no real possibility that Jill will accept the job.

(4) If there is no real possibility that Jill will accept the job, then Jill is not acting freely when she refuses the job.

Therefore

(5) If God has foreknowledge of the proposition that Jill will refuse the job before Jill is born, then Jill is not acting freely when she refuses the job.

Of course *this* argument is extremely limited in scope, applying merely to one action performed by a single person. Nevertheless the argument is instructive. For if *this* argument is sound, then it seems that our atheist can construct a similar argument when it comes to *any* action performed by *any* person. Such arguments appear to show that divine foreknowledge and human freedom cannot be reconciled. Since—as atheists will be anxious to point out—people *are* free (do act freely), it seems that we must reject belief in divine foreknowledge. Given the further assumption that God has such knowledge if God exists, the atheist can then conclude that it is not true that God exists.

10.5   A Problem for Leibniz

Should we accept this? Although I think our atheist may be on to something, the argument as it presently stands will not do. To see why, we need to consider Leibniz's thesis that "All existences, the existence of God alone excepted, are contingent."[6] Setting aside the claim that God's existence is not contingent (which we will consider in the next chapter), Leibniz is here saying that the world might not be such that you exist, or I exist, or Richard Nixon exists. (There are possible unactualized worlds in which you, I, and Nixon never exist.) This seems right. But if so, true propositions saying that you did something or that I did something (or that Nixon bombed Cambodia) cannot be *necessary* for Leibniz. Since Nixon does not bomb Cambodia in possible worlds wherein Nixon does not exist, the concession that there are possible worlds in which Nixon does not exist implies that there are possible worlds in which Nixon does not bomb Cambodia—which means that it is not *necessary* that Nixon bomb Cambodia. For similar reasons, Leibniz cannot be committed to saying that it is necessary that Jill refuses the job. The world might have been such that it is not true that Jill refuses the job, since the world might have been such that Jill never exists at all. (If there is no Jill, Jill cannot refuse or accept any job.)

   This might seem to allow Leibniz to say that people act freely. Since contingently true propositions are true propositions that might not have been true, Leibniz can correctly argue that the contingency of Jill's existence establishes that it is only contingently true and not necessarily true that Jill refuses the job. Since it is not necessary that Jill refuse the job, there is no apparent reason to deny that Jill acts freely when she refuses the job.

   Unhappily this raises a further difficulty for Leibniz. Assuming that all a priori truths are necessary truths, it follows from the denial that it is a necessary truth that Jill refuses the job that it is not an a priori truth that Jill refuses the job. Since only a priori truths can be known a priori, it follows from this that even God cannot know a priori that Jill will refuse the job. (Jack's knowledge that Jill will refuse is not a priori—it is based upon observing Jill and thereby knowing various things about Jill's character and her desires.) But if God cannot know a priori that Jill will refuse the job, that Nixon will bomb Cambodia, that you will read this book (and so on), then Leibniz has not succeeded in reconciling human free will and divine foreknowledge after all.[7]

Followers of Leibniz might reply as follows: An omnipotent (all-powerful) and omniscient (all-knowing) being has only to *decide* that something will be the case to be certain that it *will* be the case. Since God is an omnipotent and omniscient being, God has only to decide that Jill will exist to be certain that Jill will exist. In the act of deciding which of countless possible worlds to create—to make the actual world—God is in effect deciding which individuals among the countless *possible* individuals will exist. Having made this decision, God can be perfectly certain at the time the world is created that Caesar, Nixon, and Jill will exist. The real question is: How does even God know in advance, at the time of creation, say, what is true of each individual who will exist? God could hardly know that the world he is creating is the *best* of all the possible worlds that might be created unless he knows everything that subsequently will happen in the world that *is* created. But how can even God know a priori that Jill will resign if it is not necessarily true that Jill will resign?

It might be proposed that God's knowledge is rather like the knowledge a scriptwriter has concerning the plot of the story he or she creates. We ask the scriptwriter: "How do you know what happens next?" In reply, we are told "It is my story, I *decide* what happens next." Scriptwriters obviously do not have to worry about *discovering* how the story goes. A character's fate in the story is a matter of *decision* on the part of the person who makes up the story and not a matter for discovery.

The trouble with this is that characters in fictional stories are not really *free* to decide what they do. (It is the author, Joseph Heller, and not the fictional character, Yossarian, who decides what Yossarian will do next in the story.) The model of God as scriptwriter of the history of the world we inhabit is not likely to be reconciled with the fact or assumption that people act freely. Leibnizians will have to do better than this if they hope to account for human freedom.

Is there really a problem here? This might be denied. If Jack can know that Jill will refuse the job, then how can there be a problem when it comes to the hypothesis that *God* knows that Jill will refuse the job? Surely God, an alleged omniscient being, can know things ordinary people can know.

This ignores the fact that Jack's knowledge is *empirical*—is based upon observation of Jill's actions and her character. God's knowledge that Jill will refuse the job cannot be like this at all, since God knows that Jill will refuse the job long before there is a Jill (at the time of creation).

10.6   The Appeal to Conceptual Truth

Leibniz occupies a deservedly prominent place in the history of philosophy. No theorist of his stature could have been unaware of the present problem. Leibniz's proposal for resolving the problem is very ingenious and very subtle. The best that can be done here is to give the general idea behind the proposed resolution.

Leibniz believes that for each individual that will exist in the world God creates (the best of all possible worlds, according to Leibniz), there is a unique *concept* that God apprehends before the time of creation. It is because God has knowledge concerning such concepts that God is in a position to know, even before the time of creation, such ("conceptual") truths as the following:

C: If Caesar exists, then Caesar will cross the Rubicon.

N: If Nixon exists, then Nixon will resign as president.

J: If Jill exists, then Jill will refuse the job.

Each of these conditional (If, then) statements is known a priori and so is a *necessary* truth. But even though statement C is a necessary truth, neither "Caesar exists" nor "Caesar will cross the Rubicon" is a necessary truth. It is possible that there could be a world in which Caesar does not exist: therefore there could be a world in which Caesar never crosses the Rubicon. Thus from the fact that a conditional statement such as C is necessarily true, we cannot conclude that either of the component statements in C is a necessary truth.

The so-called antecedents of the conditional statements listed above are:

CE: Caesar exists.

NE: Nixon exists.

JE: Jill exists.

Each such statement is equivalent to a statement about an abstract and eternal object called an *individual concept.* We encountered concepts in the first chapter of this book. A concept C is said to be *instantiated* if and only if at least one individual *falls under* (answers to) concept C. (A concept is *uniquely* instantiated if and only if exactly one—one and only one—individual falls under this concept.) It might appear that when we make statements such as CE we are saying something about a certain individual. But perhaps appearances are misleading here. Perhaps when we assert statement CE we are really saying that a certain eternal concept is (or will be) uniquely instantiated. If we let the expression "CAESAR" name God's concept of Caesar, a Leibnizian might argue that statement CE is equivalent to:

CE*:   The concept CAESAR is (or will be) uniquely instantiated.

The attraction of this move is precisely that it offers a potential explanation of God's a priori knowledge (at the time of creation) concerning Caesar. Such knowledge cannot "latch onto" Caesar at the time of creation precisely because there is no such individual as Caesar at this time. God's a priori knowledge is in effect knowledge that concerns eternal abstract objects called *concepts* and not (directly) knowledge that is focused on *individuals.*

Each concept might be viewed as a conjunction of *qualities* or *attributes.* Thus the general concept "BACHELOR" expressed by the word "bachelor" might be viewed as the conjunction of the quality of being human, being male, being unmarried, being an adult, and so on. Note that BACHELOR (the concept) does not itself *have* (instantiate) the qualities in question. As an abstract and eternal object, BACHELOR is not itself something that is a male human being. The quality of being a male human is a *component* of the concept BACHELOR but does not *instantiate* this concept.

Unlike the concept expressed by the word "bachelor," so-called "individual" concepts are instantiated by at most one individual. This is true of the concepts "CAESAR," "NIXON," and "JILL"—the concepts associated respectively with the names "Caesar," "Nixon," "Jill." Nevertheless, such individual concepts resemble general concepts such as "BACHELOR" and "TRIANGLE" in being analyzable in terms of conjunctions of qualities. The quality of being a man is "built into" the concept "CAESAR." To really grasp the concept in question, we must know that any individual who answers to or falls under this concept must have the quality of being a man. (Again, the concept does not have this quality; any individual who falls under the concept must have this quality.) Leibniz tells us that:

> An affirmation is true if its predicate is in its subject; thus in every true affirmative proposition . . . the concept of the predicate is somehow contained in the concept of the subject, in such a way that anyone who understood the two concepts as God understands them would . . . perceive that the predicate is in the subject.[8]

God's advance knowledge of statements such as C, N, and J is in effect based upon knowledge that certain qualities are built into certain individual concepts. You and I know in advance that if there are any triangles on a certain blackboard (if the concept TRIANGLE is instantiated by any individual on a certain blackboard), then something on this blackboard must be three-sided. In much the same way, God knows in advance that if the concept "CAESAR" is instantiated, then some individual must cross the Rubicon. The qualities built into the concept "CAESAR" are in a sense definitive of what it is *to be Caesar.* Leibniz holds that everything that is true of Caesar is such that it is built into "CAESAR." It is precisely because this is so that God can have advance knowledge of propositions such as C above. No ordinary person can have a comprehensive grasp of what is built into such a concept. Only God can have such knowledge of an individual concept.

10.7   A Brief Argument in Behalf of Incompatibilism

That is, at any rate, the *general* idea. The question is: Does Leibniz's conceptual account of divine foreknowledge allow us to say that people act freely? There is much to be said about this, and unhappily I cannot pursue the matter in any detail here. But let me conclude by briefly indicating why I suspect that our question must be answered in the negative.

The argument can be posed in terms of Jill's decision to refuse the job offer. Since it is true that Jill refuses, the quality of refusing the job is for Leibniz something that is built into the concept "JILL." It is because God has perfect knowledge of this concept at the time the world is created (long before Jill herself exists) that God can know at this time that proposition J is true. J does not just *happen* to be true. J is a necessary and not a contingent truth—a truth that simply could not fail to be true.

But consider the following:

(1) If J is necessarily true, then there is no possible world in which Jill accepts the job offer.

(2) If there is no possible world in which Jill accepts the job offer, then it is not true that Jill *can* accept the job offer.

(3) If it is not true that Jill can accept the job offer, then Jill is not acting freely when she refuses the job offer.

Therefore

(4) If J is necessarily true, then Jill is not acting freely when she refuses the job offer.

Leibniz is committed to saying that J *is* necessarily true. If the present argument is sound, as I think it is, this means that Leibniz is (contrary to what he himself thinks) committed to denying that Jill acts freely when she refuses the job. But a similar argument can be constructed in the case of any action performed at any time by any person. So I think we have reason to doubt that Leibniz and his followers are in a position to account for the apparent fact that we often act freely.

CHAPTER 11

God

> . . . anyone who is interested in the question of the existence of God has to study first the divine attributes; for to say that God exists is to say that there is something that has the divine attributes; and if "God exists" is to be true, then the divine attributes must at least themselves be coherent and jointly compatible. The coherence of the notion of God, as possessor of the traditional divine attributes, is a necessary, though of course not sufficient, condition for God's existence.
>
> ANTHONY KENNY, *THE GOD OF THE PHILOSOPHERS* (1986)[1]

11.1 Divine Comfort

Many people are somehow comforted by the thought that God exists. To be sure, different people have different gods—are comforted by the thought of different gods existing. In what follows, I will confine attention to one conception of God, one divine concept, according to which God—if there is such a being—is the possessor of all and only qualities that make for *perfection*. Precisely what qualities these are is a matter of some dispute, as is the question of whether any existing being *has* (instantiates) the qualities in question. I will assume that the existence question is equivalent to the question of whether a certain *concept* traditionally associated with the word "God" is *instantiated*. To say that triangles exist is to say that the concept "TRIANGLE" is in fact instantiated. In this respect, God and triangles are in the same boat. God exists if and only if the concept "GOD" (one such concept, anyway) is instantiated. Of course there is a difference between the two cases. The difference is that while "TRIANGLE" may be and is multiply instantiated—instantiated by more than one individual—"God" is, if instantiated at all, *uniquely* instantiated—that is, instantiated by one and only one individual.

I suspect that the fact that people are comforted by the thought of God existing tells us something about the content of the concept "GOD." Many people who live impoverished lives, and who are treated unjustly, believe in God. Conceivably this belief is comforting because it reflects the conviction that any individual who answers to the concept "GOD" must be such that this individual will in the end somehow *set things right,* see to it that people receive their due or just rewards. What lies beyond such a conviction, presumably, is the conception of God as fundamentally *good.* But of course there is, conceptually speaking, more to it than that. Individuals who are good but also weak can hardly be assumed to set things right. Similarly for individuals who are both good and strong but not very *perceptive* or very *knowing.* The fact that countless people are comforted by the thought that God will in the end set things right—replace injustice and undeserved suffering with just rewards—suggests that there is a conception of God according to which God is a being supernaturally endowed with knowledge, power, and moral perfection. But to say this much is not to say or assume that God *exists.* God exists if and only if the concept "GOD" is instantiated. Since neither you nor I have the qualities of supernatural power, knowledge, and goodness, neither you nor I instantiate such a concept. Presumably no individual we have ever observed fills the bill—has the qualities in question. This raises a serious problem: If we cannot directly observe God—cannot *see* God in any literal sense—what reason can we possibly have for believing that God exists? What reason can we have for believing that the concept "GOD" is such that some existing individual answers to it?

Some people will be offended by the very suggestion that we need *reasons* for believing that God exists. It is a free country, so we can believe what we want, right? As was noted in Chapter 1, there is a sense in which this is right and a sense in which this is wrong. You *can* believe what you want in the sense that you will not be breaking any laws or be liable to prosecution. But you cannot rationally believe whatever you please without having a legitimate, rational justification for so doing. (I might believe that I can fly to Denver under my own power, but such a belief is hardly justifiable rationally.)

11.2   Natural Design

Suppose that Jack suffers serious injuries in a car accident and is for many weeks confined to a hospital room without windows. One day

Jack's friend Jill comes to visit. Jack notices that Jill's raincoat and hat that are covered with water. What accounts for this? Jack might entertain different hypotheses, each of which purports to explain the wet raingear. One such hypothesis is that the doctors and nurses Jill passed in the hallway are playing with water pistols and that Jill got into the line of fire. Another is that the sprinkler system in the hallway is malfunctioning. Still another that it is raining outside. Somehow this last hypothesis seems the *best explanation* of what Jack sees. (Precisely why one hypothesis offers the best explanation of the observed "data" is a complicated question that is not addressed here.) The case is instructive because it suggests that Jack is *justified* in believing that it is raining outside even though he cannot directly *observe* this. Jack's justification for believing this rests with the fact, as I take it to be, that the best explanation for what he observes (Jill's wet raingear) states that it *is* raining outside. Arguably this model of "indirect" justification for belief carries over to the case of belief in God's existence. We cannot directly observe God in the way we can (on some accounts) observe tables, chairs, and mountains. Still, perhaps what we *can* observe is best explained by the hypothesis that God exists.

Many theorists have argued that this is so. Let us briefly consider one such argument, advanced by an imaginary philosopher named Cleanthes in *Dialogues Concerning Natural Religion,* a work by David Hume published in 1779. Cleanthes asks us to do the following:

> Look round the world, contemplate the whole and every part of it: you will find it to be nothing but one great machine, subdivided into an infinite number of lesser machines, which again admit of subdivisions to a degree beyond what human senses and faculties can trace and explain. All these various machines, and even their most minute parts, are adjusted to each other with an accuracy which ravishes into admiration all men who have ever contemplated them. The curious adapting of means to ends, throughout all nature, resembles exactly, though it much exceeds, the production of human contrivance—of human design, thought, wisdom, and intelligence. Since therefore the effects resemble each other, we are led to infer, by all the rules of analogy, that the causes also resemble, and that the Author of nature is somewhat similar to the mind of man, though possessed of much larger faculties. . . .[2]

Cleanthes is not to be taken literally when he speaks of the natural world as "one great machine." His point, as I interpret it, is that the natural world is *like* a machine in the sense that its various parts (and parts of these parts) interact in an intricate and even mathematically precise manner. As aspiring makers of artificial hearts have discovered, natural objects such as the human heart are incredibly efficient performers of tasks that are essential to wholes (the human body, in the case of the heart) whereof they are components. Cleanthes speaks not of the heart but of the eye in this context:

> Consider, anatomize the eye, survey its structure and contrivance, and tell me, from our own feeling, if the idea of a contriver does not immediately flow in upon you with a force like that of sensation. The most obvious conclusion, surely, is in favor of design. . . .[3]

The idea of designing and producing artificial eyes that function as well as the natural human eye is a daunting prospect, to say the least.

One might ask what all of this has to do with *God*. The general idea, I think, is something like this: Similar effects suggest, make reasonable the assumption of, similar causes. Natural objects such as the human eye (heart, etc.) are similar to artifacts such as bridges and clocks with respect to the fact that their various parts interact in precise and complicated ways to produce results that are essential to the whole whereof they are parts. Since we know that bridges and clocks are produced by intelligent beings who have consciously *designed* the objects they produce, we thus have reason to believe that natural objects are similarly produced by design and so produced by an intelligent being. Since no *human* being designed and produced the natural objects that make up the natural world, Cleanthes concludes that the best hypothesis is that the natural world was produced by a supernatural being possessed of "much larger faculties" than human designers. Cleanthes calls this being "God."

Although some people find this convincing, I believe that the argument is unsound. Part of the problem lies with the premise that similar effects license the conclusion of similar causes. As Cleanthes' critics are quick to point out, there is a sense in which a spider's web is similar to man-made things such as intricate pathways in a garden or an airport terminal. We know that the pathways and the terminal are designed by intelligent beings. However, we can hardly conclude that the web is produced by an intelligent being. The fact that there are similarities between the web and the garden pathway (or airport terminal) does not make reasonable the assumption that the causes are similar in the two cases. So Cleanthes' argument rests upon at least one false assumption. (As one critic observes, it is difficult to see why "an orderly system may not be spun from the belly as well as the brain."[4] Even if the argument's premises were true, it is not at all clear that anything Cleanthes says supports any conception of God that will be comforting to the downtrodden. For all Cleanthes says, the natural world might have been designed by a team of supernatural beings who are entirely indifferent to human suffering and the achievement of ultimate justice for oppressed people. If our conception of God is the conception of a being who will make things right, we need to look elsewhere for an argument supporting the hypothesis that God exists.

Of course there is much more to be said concerning appeals to design. I suspect that in the end all such arguments in behalf of God will look rather problematic. Biologists will argue that evolutionary facts concerning "natural selection" can best account for the intricate structure of the human eye. If the biological argument is sound, as it seems to be, we should reject the proposal that the hypothesis of God's existence offers the best explanation of the design of the eye.[5]

11.3   Ontological Arguments

Some theorists deny that the case for God's existence must rest upon "best hypothesis of what we observe" arguments. Such theorists maintain that purely *conceptual* considerations—facts concerning the concept (one traditional concept) expressed by the word "God"—will supply overwhelmingly good if not decisive reasons for judging that God exists. Let us call such arguments *ontological* arguments for the existence of God. There are many arguments of this sort. Descartes is formulating one of these when he observes:

> I assuredly find in myself the idea of God—of a supremely perfect being—no less than the idea of a figure or a number; and I clearly and distinctly understand that everlasting existence belongs to his nature, no less than I can see that what I prove of some figure, or number, belongs to the nature of that

> figure, or number. So . . . I ought to hold the existence of God
> with at least the same degree of certainty as I have so far held
> mathematical truths.[6]

Note that Descartes does not focus attention upon things he sees
around him but rather upon something he finds in himself, an
"idea" or more properly a *concept*. The general thrust of the argument is that by examining this concept ("GOD"), we can prove
nonempirically, without recourse to our perceptual faculties, that
God exists. Descartes seems to assume that it is a conceptual truth
that God is supremely perfect. Given the further premise that anything that is supremely perfect is such that it exists, it follows that
God exists. The argument seems to have this form:

(1) God is supremely perfect.

(2) If God is supremely perfect, then God exists.

Therefore

(3) God exists.

We might have reservations about this. In particular, we may ask
what justification Descartes has for (1). Just as Santa Claus does not
really have the quality of being fat or being an owner of a sleigh
unless Santa really exists, God does not have any qualities and so
does not have the quality of being supremely perfect (whatever
quality this is) *unless* God exists. Descartes seems to be *begging the
question*—assuming the truth of the very point he is out to prove—
when he asserts (1). Unless we *first* have reason to believe that God
exists, we can hardly be assured that God has the quality of being
supremely perfect. Nonexisting things simply do not have any qualities or attributes. Unless we first know that (3) is true, we are in no
position to claim to know that (1) is true. So the truth of (3) is hardly
established by an appeal to (1) and (2).

Defenders of Descartes might reply that (1) is established by
reflecting upon the concept "GOD." Just as the quality of being
three-sided is built into the concept "TRIANGLE," the quality of
being supremely perfect is built into the concept "GOD." From this
it might be concluded that we have good (conceptual) reason to
accept (1) after all.

It is important to see not only that this line of argument is
fallacious but also *why* it is fallacious. The fallacy lies with the as-

sumption that because a quality is built into a certain concept, this quality must be instantiated (must apply to some individual). This assumption is mistaken, as we can see when we examine the concept expressed by the term "Superman." It is true that the quality of being a person who can fly through the air under his own power is built into the concept "SUPERMAN." But it does not follow from this—indeed, it is false—that any individual really has (instantiates) this quality. No individual falls under the concept "SUPERMAN" (Superman does not exist).

Of course this might be challenged. Conceivably someone might argue as follows:

(1*) If Superman exists, then Superman (really) has the quality of being a person who can fly under his own power.

(2*) Superman exists.

Therefore

(3*) Superman really has the quality of being a person who can fly under his own power.

Perhaps sober reflection on the concept "SUPERMAN" will assure us that premise (1*) is true. Even if that is so, premise (2*) is false (Superman does not exist). The point is worth keeping in mind when we consider the further argument:

(1**) If God exists, then God really has the quality of being supremely perfect.

(2**) God exists.

Therefore

(3**) God really has the quality of being supremely perfect.

Here the situation differs from the Superman case, since it is not *clear* whether God exists or not. But to say that God's existence is in doubt is to say that premise (2**) is in doubt, which means that the present argument is inconclusive *even if it is true* that reflection upon the concept "GOD" assures us that (1**) is true. The crucial point, in short, is that we cannot conclude from the examination of any concept that any individual has the quality of being supremely perfect. Therefore even if existence is required of any individual who is supremely perfect, we as yet have no real reason to believe that God exists.

11.4   A Revised Ontological Argument

Perhaps theists (people who believe in God's existence) can do better than this. Let us grant Descartes's point that the concept "GOD" is the concept of a supremely perfect being. What is involved in supreme perfection? Presumably a supremely perfect individual has no imperfections. Assuming that it is *possible* that the concept "GOD" is instantiated, then it must at least be possible that some individual has no imperfections at all. If we agree with this possibility claim, we may believe that there is a clear and forceful line of argument in support of God's existence.

The argument is based upon the idea that "a being whose nonexistence is logically impossible is 'greater' than a being whose nonexistence is logically possible."[7] This takes some explaining. Let us say that an individual has the property of being *necessary* if and only if this individual could not fail to be part of the real world. (Individuals that are part of the world but that fail to be necessary are said to be *contingent.*) Since the Eiffel Tower might very well not be part of the "real world," the Eiffel Tower is a contingent and not a necessary being. Assuming that supreme perfection implies necessity, it follows that the Eiffel Tower is not supremely perfect. The Eiffel Tower is, of course, perfectly real—it is a genuine and not merely an imaginary or fictitious part of the world we inhabit. Nonetheless, the Eiffel Tower might be destroyed by a terrorist's bomb or some natural event such as an earthquake. Arguably such possibilities show that the Eiffel Tower, whatever can be said in its behalf, is not *supremely* perfect. Only a being that is truly *necessary*—a being that could not fail to be part of the real world—can qualify as supremely perfect.

Given this assumption, it might be proposed that there is a powerful argument in behalf of God's existence. The argument rests upon the following premises:

(1) Supreme perfection implies necessity (that is, no contingent being can possibly be supremely perfect).

(2) Possibly the concept GOD is instantiated.

(3) The quality of being supremely perfect is built into the concept GOD.

(2) implies that there is a possible situation (a possible world, if you will) in which some individual falls under the concept "GOD." Let us employ the term "Yahweh" to name such a hypothetical individ-

ual. By hypothesis, there is a *possible* situation in which Yahweh answers to the concept "GOD." It follows from this and (3) that:

> (4) There is a possible situation in which Yahweh is supremely perfect.

Initially this might appear harmless enough. Many things are *possible* that are not really *true*. It is possible, in some sense, for me to occupy the office of president of the United States. The mere fact that such a thing is possible does not license the conclusion that it is *true* that I am president. So how can the possibility claim in (4) tell us anything about what is true in the world we actually inhabit?

Generally, reflection upon what is merely possible does not tell us much about what *actually* is the case. But perhaps the situation is different when we consider (4). The conjunction of (4) and (1) implies that:

> (5) There is a possible situation in which Yahweh is necessary.

A *necessary* being is a being that cannot, logically, fail to exist under any circumstances. So if (5) is true, it appears that there is a possible situation in which a certain individual (Yahweh) is a necessary being and so a being that cannot fail to exist. Since a necessary being exists in *every* possible situation, it might be concluded that Yahweh must be present in the *actual* world we inhabit. Surely the way things are in the actual world we inhabit is one way, though only one way, things might be. (As followers of Leibniz put it, the actual world is one of countless possible worlds.) If Yahweh did not exist in the actual world we inhabit, Yahweh simply could not qualify as a necessary being in the (stipulated) possible circumstances in which Yahweh falls under the concept "GOD." This contradicts the assumption that no individual falls under "GOD" unless it is a necessary being.

A defender of the revised ontological argument will conclude that it follows from (1) through (5) that Yahweh is part of the world we inhabit (the actual world). Since Yahweh is God, it follows that God is part of the actual world.

11.5   Unanswered Questions

There are, however, some tough questions that confront defenders of the argument just outlined. One such question arises when we recognize that the argument tacitly assumes that if

(1) Possibly Yahweh falls under the concept GOD

and

(2) Yahweh exists in the actual world (that is, is part of the actual world),

then

(3) The concept GOD is instantiated in the actual world (that is, God exists in the actual world).

But is such an inference legitimate? I doubt that it is. Consider a parallel case. It is surely *possible* that I might be king of the United States. From this fact and the further fact that I exist in the actual world (am part of the actual world), we can hardly conclude that the concept KING OF THE UNITED STATES is instantiated in the actual world. The following argument is clearly invalid:

(1*) Possibly Carter falls under the concept KING OF THE UNITED STATES.

(2*) Carter (me) exists in the actual world.

Therefore

(3*) The concept KING OF THE UNITED STATES is instantiated in the actual world.

Quite *clearly*, (3*) is false. (No individual actually falls under the concept in question.) Equally clearly, (1*) and (2*) are true. This shows that (3*) does not follow logically from the conjunction of (1*) and (2*). But why should the situation be different when we turn to the argument that proceeds from (1) and (2) to (3)? Even if we allow that it is true that it is possible for Yahweh (a certain hypothetical individual) to fall under the concept GOD and true also that this hypothetical individual must be part of the world we actually inhabit, it simply does not follow without further assumptions that the concept GOD is instantiated in the world we actually inhabit. And since "God exists" is true if and only if this concept is instantiated, it does not follow from anything said in section 11.4 that it is true that God exists.

Some theorists will deny that this is a forceful objection to the revised ontological argument. Such theorists may insist that

> . . . there is no possible world in which an individual who is God in any world fails to exemplify one of the divine attributes, either by failing to exist, or by existing without having one of those properties.[8]

If this is right, my objection to the ontological argument misfires. But *is* it right? Let us define a *rigid* concept to be such that it *necessarily* applies to any individual to which it *possibly* applies. Quite clearly such concepts as "PRESIDENT OF THE UNITED STATES" and "KING OF ENGLAND" are not rigid in this sense. Such concepts may apply to one individual in one possible situation and to other individuals in still other possible situations. If the passage just cited is correct, the concept GOD is not like this at all. GOD is, rather, a rigid concept that applies to the same individual in different possible situations (and at different times).

I confess that I see no good reason to accept this. But for the sake of argument, let us suppose that GOD is a rigid concept. If that is true, I believe that we should question the proposal that it is even *possible* that some individual falls under the concept GOD.

Suppose that GOD is rigid and that there is a possible world in which some individual (Yahweh) falls under this concept. In the world in question, Yahweh is supremely perfect, since such perfection is required of any individual falling under GOD. Supreme perfection requires unlimited power (omnipotence). So Yahweh is in this possible world omnipotent. Since an omnipotent being can do anything an ordinary person can do, Yahweh can do anything an ordinary person can do.

Ordinary people can do—indeed, often *do* do—evil things. For example, ordinary people can maliciously inflict great pain on others for no good reason at all. As a supremely perfect and so omnipotent being, Yahweh *can* do this. But of course if Yahweh falls under GOD, Yahweh does not do any such thing. Supreme perfection involves not only unlimited power but also *moral goodness.* If Yahweh is God, then Yahweh is morally perfect. So Yahweh does not exercise his power maliciously to inflict pain on others.

The problem lies with the fact that as an omnipotent being, Yahweh can maliciously inflict pain on others. If Yahweh can do this, then there are *possible* situations (worlds) in which Yahweh *does* maliciously inflict pain on others. Given the assumption that GOD is a rigid concept, Yahweh must fall under the concept GOD even in worlds where he does the horrible things he has the power to do. But this contradicts the assumption that moral perfection is built into the concept GOD. Yahweh is hardly morally perfect in possible worlds in which he maliciously pushes children in front of trains or trucks.

A similar problem emerges when we view the situation from

a somewhat different perspective. For suppose that GOD is rigid and that Yahweh—a hypothetical individual who falls under GOD in some possible situation—is simply incapable of committing evil deeds. There is then no possible situation in which Yahweh pushes children in front of trains. This means that Yahweh *cannot* push children in front of trains. However, Yahweh can hardly be an omnipotent (all-powerful) individual if he cannot do things that ordinary people can do. Accordingly it is hard to see how Yahweh can fall under the concept GOD (since the quality of omnipotence is built into this concept).

Perhaps the point comes into clearer focus when we try to conjoin the rigidity assumption with the proposition that it is *actually* true (not just possibly true) that Yahweh falls under GOD. Suppose:

(1) GOD is a rigid concept.

(2) Yahweh actually falls under GOD.

It follows from these claims that there is no possible situation in which Yahweh fails to have the divine attributes, the various perfection-making qualities, that are built into the concept GOD. Since Yahweh is morally perfect in every possible situation, there is no possible situation in which Yahweh maliciously pushes children in front of trains. This contradicts the claim, implied by (2), that Yahweh is all-powerful. How can Yahweh be all-powerful if Yahweh cannot do things that you and I can do?

11.6   Pascal's Wager

Perhaps there are good answers to such questions. However, until such answers are forthcoming, it might appear that we do well to remain agnostic concerning the hypothesis that God exists. Relative to the evidence we possess, it seems that the *probability* that God exists is no greater than the probability that God doesn't exist. Assuming that it is rational to believe statement S if and only if the probability of S is greater than the probability of the denial of S, it follows that it is not rational to believe that God exists. Perhaps things work the same way when we consider the atheist's proposition that God does not exist. If the probability that the atheist is right is no greater than the probability that the atheist is wrong, perhaps the rational thing to do is to withhold belief entirely—to believe neither that God exists nor that God does not exist. If we do this, we are *agnostics*.

Not everyone agrees with the probability assumption that underlies the agnostic position. If we follow the French mathematician Blaise Pascal, we will deny that it is rational to believe a statement or proposition only on the condition that the probability of this proposition is greater than the probability of its negation. Consider the following situation: an eccentric multi-millionaire arranges a race between two horses, A and B. It is to be a fair race and the horses are evenly matched. Relative to the evidence we possess, the probability that A will be the winner is fifty-fifty. Is it then *irrational* to bet on horse A? Not necessarily. For suppose that our eccentric friend puts into writing (into a contract) that a winning bet on A will pay exactly 1 million dollars, while a winning bet on B will pay exactly $2. (You can only bet on one horse, and can only bet one dollar.) The situation is highly unusual, to say the least, but it is instructive—Pascal would argue—in that it demonstrates that the probabilities alone do not determine the rational course of action. The probability that you will lose, and walk away empty handed, if you bet on A is precisely the same as the probability that you will lose if you bet on B. Nonetheless, Pascal and his followers would say that the rational thing to do is to bet on horse A (and to say that it is irrational to bet on horse B).

Defenders of God might be encouraged by this. They might allow that the chances of being right—believing what is *true*—are no greater if you believe in God's existence than if you believe in God's non-existence. What makes it rational to believe in God, nonetheless, is the fact that you stand to gain more in the event that you are right. Even though you may well be wasting your time totally if you believe in God and worship God, it turns out—as followers of Pascal will insist—that it is perfectly rational to do just this.

The Pascalian line of argument is both subtle and interesting. I cannot do the argument justice here. I can only say that insofar as we undertake to formulate a representation of the world that is *true*—one that represents things as they are—I see at present no justification for believing that God exists.

Being Realistic

Realism is a declaration of independence. . . . Realists from Plato onward have argued that man is *not* the measure of all things.

ELLIOT SOBER, "REALISM AND INDEPENDENCE" (1982)[1]

How could there be only one true and complete description of the way the world is? The concepts we use in describing the world are not inevitable.

HARTREY FIELD, "REALISM AND RELATIVISM" (1982)[2]

12.1   The Limits of Common Sense

Each of us has a distinctive way of viewing the world we inhabit, a distinctive *representation* of it. As noted at the outset, such a representation is a system of beliefs. Metaphysicians are not alone in debating questions as to *which* beliefs do and do not belong in an accurate or realistic representation of the world. Attentive readers may have concluded that my own belief system is one that does not picture an existing God, that rejects both the idealist view (that tables and trees are collections of ideas) and the dualist view (that our minds are spiritual rather than material substances), and that endorses the idea that people often act freely and bear responsibility for their actions notwithstanding the fact that people are material substances and the further fact that every action and every decision for which any person bears responsibility has a cause. It goes without saying that this metaphysical system will strike some people as fundamentally misguided in one or more than one way. Perhaps the critics are right. Certainly I am prepared to *alter* my representation of the world in the face of persuasive arguments opposing one or more of my metaphysical beliefs or showing that my belief system suffers from inconsistency. At present, I fail to see that there are such arguments. But I recognize that such arguments may possibly be presented to me. If this happens, I will revise my belief system accordingly.

If we are *realists,* we will allow that the world is one thing and our representation of the world—our system of beliefs about it—is quite another. Ideally we seek to attain a representation of the world that is as comprehensive and as accurate as possible. But how are we to do this? How should a rational person proceed in confronting metaphysical questions that bear upon the general nature of the world we inhabit?

Philosophers such as Moore place great stock upon common sense. But this raises questions. Precisely what are we appealing to when we appeal to common sense? How are we to decide whether common sense gives its seal of approval to a metaphysical thesis? Consider the question of God's existence. Does common sense have anything to say here? If we follow the dictates of common sense, will we believe that God exists? Moore maintains that "On the whole, I think it fairest to say that Common Sense has *no* view on the question whether we do know that there is a God or not: that it neither asserts that we do know this, nor yet that we do not. . . ."[3] Note that this does not answer our question. We may grant this— grant that common sense says nothing about *knowing* that God exists—and still wonder whether common sense supports the view that *God exists.*

Moore goes on to say that "enormous numbers of people, and not philosophers only, believe that there certainly is a God in the Universe." Can common sense then *not* support the view that God exists? If we think that anything believed by enormous numbers of people must be a matter of common sense, then we will be hard-pressed to deny that the God hypothesis is supported by common sense. So what? It seems to me that, if common sense is determined merely on the basis of what everyone or nearly everyone believes, there is very little hope for the Moorean proposal that common sense should be our guide when we encounter metaphysical issues. Perhaps it is true that nearly everyone believes in an afterlife. If *this* means that common sense licenses such a belief, then we should not assume that common sense offers even a remotely reliable guide to metaphysical issues.[4]

We have seen that some metaphysical arguments speak in behalf of conclusions that are deeply *revisionistic*—that conflict sharply with our normal way of viewing the world. It is not unlikely that appeals to common sense will generally reflect a bias on behalf of the conceptual status quo—our established way of viewing things. The plain fact is, however, that our established way of viewing the world may in certain instances *require* revision. Scientific discoveries may reveal that "commonsense" beliefs should be rejected. Let us consider, again very briefly, one illustration of this. Jules and Jim are twins. When Jules is sent on a mission to Alpha Centauri, Jim remains behind on earth. Jules's spacecraft travels with half the velocity of light and the round trip takes, by Jim's calendar, sixteen years. Question: Is Jules older than, younger than, or the same age as Jim upon his return to earth?

Common sense says that if X and Y are the same age at one time then X and Y are forever the same age—or the same age for as long as X and Y exist. However, work in theoretical physics suggests that common sense is mistaken in judging that Jules and Jim are the same age when Jules returns. If the *experts* are right, Jules is more than two years younger than Jim when he returns. Even though Jules and Jim are born at the same time, it comes to happen that Jim is considerably older than Jim. I shall not attempt to explain *why* things are said to work this way. (That story is too long and complicated to be told here.[5]) For present purposes, the important thing is that the common-sense view of the situation is in conflict with the facts as the "facts" are depicted by the experts. The point is *not* that the experts must be right. Conceivably some horrible though subtle mistake underlies the reasoning of the experts. Things might turn out this way. But it may also turn out that the experts *are* right and common sense is wrong. Certainly it will not do simply to assume as an article of faith that "common sense" can never play us false. If we take common sense as an endorsement of everything that is generally believed, the history of thought will show us conclusively that common sense is frequently unrealistic. As Michael Dummett observes, "common sense always lags behind scientific theory."[6] Of course, physical theory is one thing and metaphysical theory another (yet closely related) thing. But given that common sense is so often wrong when it comes to physical theory, one may well ask why common sense should be our guide in metaphysics.

12.2   Two Conceptions of Truth

To the extent that a representation of the world is accurate, this system contains *true* beliefs. As noted at the outset of this book, the subject of truth generates a great deal of metaphysical controversy. We might say that a *true* statement or belief is such that it represents the world as it really is. What is meant by "the world as it really is"? In a famous book entitled *Tractatus Logico-Philosophicus*, Ludwig Wittgenstein argues that:

> The world is the totality of facts, not of things.[7]

What is Wittgenstein driving at here? Perhaps an example will help. We might know that there is a city called Seattle and another called Denver and still not know whether Seattle's population is larger than that of Denver. To the extent that we do not know what the *fact* of the matter is with respect to the comparative sizes of the two cities, we fail to know what our world is like. More generally, a knowledge of what things there are in the world does not suffice to tell us what the world is like. The world is the sum or totality of all the facts concerning all the things there are and not merely the sum or totality of all the things there are. Wittgenstein is talking about the *actual* world. No possible world that is unrealized is a totality of facts. Unrealized possible worlds consist of states of affairs that fail to be but might have been facts. (Such is the case with the state of affairs wherein Michael Dukakis is elected president.)

On one account of truth, a true statement or belief is such that it *corresponds to a fact.* You might for some reason believe that I was once on the U.S. Olympic Ski Team. Since it is not a fact that I *was* on the team, your belief fails to be true. The *correspondence theory of truth* sounds plausible enough, but it is not without critics.

One argument opposing the correspondence theory proceeds as follows: If we try to explain truth in terms of correspondence with facts, then we must be prepared to explain what *facts* are. Unhappily, we cannot give an account, in a way that is unbiased and perfectly objective, of the facts that collectively make up the actual world. There is simply no saying what the facts are apart from a certain *conceptual* vantage point. Since different observers may employ different conceptual schemes, different observers will give somewhat different accounts of the "facts." In short, there simply is no such thing as *the* (unique) way the world is. The way the world is (the facts) is relative to our conceptual outlook. As Hilary Putnam argues:

> If the notion of comparing our system of beliefs with uncon-
> ceptualized reality to see if they match makes no sense, then
> the claim that science seeks to discover the truth can mean
> no more than that science seeks to construct a world picture
> which, in the ideal limit, satisfies certain criteria of rational
> acceptability.[8]

This suggests an alternative to the correspondence theory, namely, that a statement is *true* if and only if we are (or would be in "the ideal limit") *rationally justified or warranted in asserting* this statement. Let us call this *the warrant theory* of truth. Unlike the correspondence theory, the warrant theory does not presuppose that facts are independent of concepts. As the passage just cited suggests, warrant theorists are skeptical of the suggestion that there is such a thing as "unconceptualized reality."

Various objections may be presented against the warrant theory of truth. Suppose that Jack, who has not had a medical examination in many years, has bone cancer. Since Jack's disease has not yet caused any observable symptoms, it seems that no one is justified or warranted in asserting that Jack has bone cancer. Nonetheless it is *true* that Jack has bone cancer. Thus we seem to have discovered a case wherein we have truth without warranted (justified) assertability. Such a case may suggest that the warrant theory must be mistaken.

This objection is based upon a misinterpretation of the warrant theorist's position. The position is, roughly, that truth is what we would be warranted in asserting in *ideal* circumstances—roughly, circumstances where we have gathered all the evidence there is to gather. Since we have not gathered all the evidence there is to gather in Jack's case, the fact that we are not warranted in asserting the true statement that Jack has bone cancer does not serve to refute the warrant theory.

There are, however, worrisome cases that are not so easily dismissed. Recently Hartrey Field has argued that "there seems to be good reason to reject the equation of truth with idealized rational acceptability."[9] Field rests his case with dinosaurs. The number of dinosaurs that existed is (we assume) not greater than 100^{10}. Given this fact, Field argues that exactly one of the following statements must be true:

> There were exactly zero dinosaurs,
> There was exactly one dinosaur,
> There were exactly two dinosaurs,
> . . . .
> There were exactly 100^{10} dinosaurs.

If truth were idealized rational acceptability, then we would in ideal circumstances be rationally warranted in accepting one (and only one) of these statements. Field argues that this is not so. Even if we conduct an exhaustive study of all the evidence there is to examine, we will not be rationally warranted in asserting any statement on the above list. Since one (we know not which) such statement is *true*, Field concludes that truth cannot be equated with idealized rational acceptability.

12.3   Does Bivalence Hold for "God Exists"?

It is not entirely clear how warrant theorists are to reply to Field's objection in the dinosaur case. One possible reply is to argue that this challenge fails for the same reason that the bone cancer example fails: in neither case are we presently in an ideal position when it comes to making judgments. In the dinosaur case, the *ideal* situation is one in which there is today available evidence that tells us precisely how many dinosaurs once existed. Since we are not in this situation, the fact that we are not presently warranted in asserting any of the statements on Field's list does not imply (on the warrant theory of truth) that no such statement is true.

But we may have reservations about this defense. Is it not in some cases possible that even the *best evidence we possibly could have* will not decide the question at hand—will not even give us rational warrant or justification for making a judgment one way or the other? If the question deserves an affirmative answer, then it will hardly do to say that an ideal situation is one in which we have evidence that settles (decides) the question at hand.

Conceivably things will turn out this way with respect to the question of God's existence. Jack's and Jill's representations of the world are much the same with the exception of beliefs concerning

God. Whereas Jack (a theist) believes that God exists, Jill (an atheist) believes that God does not exist. (Let us assume both parties have the same concept of God.) Otherwise Jack and Jill have more or less the same beliefs—the same way of representing the world. Is Jack's representation then more realistic than Jill's or Jill's more realistic than Jack's? To decide this, it seems we need to know whether it is true or false that God exists.

Suppose (though many people will not be prepared to grant that this is so) that the best evidence we can possibly have will not decide the matter. What are warrant theorists to say about such a case? If neither the statement that God exists (G) nor the statement that God does not exist (NG) is rationally warranted even in "ideal" circumstances, where we have the best evidence that could be had, the warrant theory seems to imply that neither statement G nor statement NG is *true*. Can this really be right? (Can it really be right to say that neither "God exists" nor "God does not exist" is true?) We might have misgivings about this. If statement NG fails to be true, then we might believe that statement G must be true (and conversely). Warrant theorists may deny this, holding that in the event that even the best evidence that could be had does not decide the matter, neither G nor NG is a true statement. Is either statement ("God exists"/"God does not exist") then *false*? It is hard to see how the answer can be affirmative, since if either statement were false, the other would presumably be true. Given our present assumptions, it appears that it may turn out that neither G nor NG is either true or false.

There is a basic principle of logic—*the principle of bivalence*, as it is called—that says that every meaningful statement is either true or false. The bivalence principle implies—assuming that "God exists" is a meaningful statement—that it is either true or false that God exists. If we accept the bivalence principle, we will find it hard to go along with the proposal that *true* beliefs are precisely beliefs that are rationally acceptable. Conceivably it might turn out that even the best evidence (best arguments) we can have fail to decide the question of God's existence. Suppose this happens. If we equate truth and rational acceptability, then we must conclude that it is neither true nor false that God exists. I confess that I find it hard to take this seriously. Why should there not be legitimate questions having objective answers which we never, even at the ideal limit, can be rationally warranted in asserting? Presumably it can be true that there were precisely *n* dinosaurs (where *n* is some finite but perhaps large number) even though no one can be warranted in asserting that there were precisely this many dinosaurs. So why can it not be true that God does or does not exist even though no one is warranted in asserting such a claim?

12.4   Antirealist Opposition to Independence

To be a *realist* is to hold that the world is in some sense *independent* of even the most credible worldly representations. If we take "the world" to be the totality of all the *facts*, realism is the view that facts are in theory independent not only of what we believe is and is not the case but independent also of our means of verifying our beliefs. As William Alston says, "epistemic justification is intimately connected with truth; not necessarily so closely connected that justification entails truth, but at least so closely connected that justification entails a considerable probability of truth."[10] Antirealists find such independence claims problematic. (Accordingly antirealists often argue against the bivalence principle.[11]) Consider the following "science fiction possibility," constructed by Hilary Putnam in a book entitled *Reason, Truth, and History*:

> Imagine that a human being (you can imagine this to be yourself) has been subjected to an operation by an evil scientist. The person's brain (your brain) has been removed from the body and placed in a vat of nutrients which keeps the brain alive. The nerve endings have been connected to a super-scientific computer which causes the person whose brain it is to have the illusion that everything is perfectly normal. There seem to be people, objects, the sky, etc.; but really all the person (you) is experiencing is the result of electronic impulses travelling from the computer to the nerve endings. The computer is so clever that if the person tries to raise his hand, the feedback from the computer will cause him to "see" and "feel" the hand being raised. Moreover, by varying the program, the evil scientist can cause the victim to "experience" (or hallucinate) any situation or environment the evil scientist wishes.[12]

Putnam argues that a proper understanding of the implications of the brain-in-the-vat hypothesis will serve to discredit realism. In barest outline, the argument seems to have this form:

(1) If realism were correct, the brain-in-the-vat hypothesis would in theory be possible.

(2) The brain-in-the-vat hypothesis is not in theory possible (It is a "self-refuting" hypothesis).

Therefore

(3) Realism is not correct.[13]

Putnam's reasons in behalf of premise (2) are too complex to consider here. But let me make one or two observations concerning his case in support of premise (1). On Putnam's analysis, defenders of "metaphysical realism" hold that the "the world consists of some fixed totality of mind-independent objects."[14] If we follow Wittgenstein, we might say that such "objects" are *facts.* But what sort of thing, exactly, *is* a fact? Moore assures us that facts are "the sort of entities which *correspond* . . . to true beliefs."[15] Beliefs, which in some sense have concepts as constituents, are somehow *in* the mind, whereas *facts*—things that collectively make up the world—are not in the mind. On this realist assessment of the situation, it is in theory possible that the world (the facts) could be radically different from our representation of it. As Putnam observes, for realists:

> THE WORLD is supposed to be *independent* of any particular representation we have of it—indeed, it is held that we might be *unable* to represent THE WORLD correctly at all (e.g. we might all be "brains in a vat," the metaphysical realist tells us).[16]

Putnam argues, in effect, that if we are metaphysical realists, we must allow that the vat hypothesis is in theory possible. Since, as Putnam further argues, this hypothesis is *not* possible, we have good reason to reject metaphysical realism. Contrary to what realists believe, facts simply are not mind-independent. According to Putnam, "A fact is something it is rational to believe."[17]

The battle between realists and antirealists is going on today. Quite clearly, the outcome of this controversy will have implications for many if not all of the questions addressed in this book. Antirealists are likely to argue for a negative answer to the meta-metaphysical question "Do metaphysical questions have uniquely correct answers?" As Putnam asks:

> . . . why should there not sometimes be equally coherent but incompatible conceptual schemes which fit our experiential be-

liefs equally well? If truth is not (unique) correspondence, then the possibility of a certain pluralism is opened up. But the motive of the metaphysical realist is to save the notion of the God's Eye Point of View, i.e. the One True Theory.[18]

If Putnam is right about this, there may be no uniquely correct representation of the world, no uniquely correct answer to some or all of the metaphysical questions we have addressed. I have no decisive argument opposing the antirealist's pluralism. But I confess to skepticism, believing as I do that there are many facts for which we will never have an even remotely plausible rational justification and many metaphysical questions having only one correct answer.

I think we know very well that we are not brains in a vat. For all we know, it is not *epistemically* possible that we are brains in a vat. Nonetheless there may be a broader sense of possibility in which the vat hypothesis *is* possible. If I know that my dog is lying under the table, then it is not epistemically possible that the dog is not presently under the table. Nonetheless there is a sense in which it is possible (logically possible, perhaps one should say) that the dog is not presently under the table. My knowledge of the dog's location involves *justification* for believing that the dog is in a certain place. But such justification does not logically guarantee the *truth* of what is believed. Contrary to what antirealists say, there appears to be a logical gap between justification and truth.

12.5   In Behalf of Metaphysics

Whatever truth is, it certainly is hard to come by. It is hard enough to keep track of one's bank account or tax-return forms much less to resolve rationally the large questions addressed in the preceding discussion. Would it not be best not even to *consider* metaphysical questions? It is not clear that this is a real possibility for most of us. Hume correctly observed that " 'tis almost impossible for the mind of man to rest, like those of beasts, in that narrow circle of objects, which are the subject of daily conversation and action. . . ."[19] When we venture out of such a narrow circle, we unavoidably come up against metaphysical issues. Metaphysical questions are not to everyone's taste. Nonetheless, I believe that metaphysical curiosity is a worthy and even sometimes noble human characteristic. There is something very sad about the spectacle of people who are so preoccupied with the "narrow circle of objects, which are the subject of daily conversation and action" that they never pause to reflect upon their own nature and that of the world they inhabit. We can hardly avoid having *some* representation of ourselves and our world. Metaphysical reasoning begins when we consider the fact that there are in theory a great many conflicting representations of the world and proceed critically to examine and compare the various alternatives. I grant that the preceding discussion does not take us far toward a deep and comprehensive understanding of these matters. However, I hope enough has been said to encourage readers to take stock of their favored view of the world and to consider the possibility that this representation may, in some respects, be in need of revision. I hope, too, that no one will seriously entertain the hypothesis that there are as many worlds as there are representations of it—and that there are therefore no uniquely correct answers to metaphysical questions.

I conclude with an autobiographical remark: My own representation of the world is in a distressing number of ways incomplete and in many ways in transition. However, some of my metaphysical beliefs seem to me both well-founded and unlikely to require revision. We are surrounded by things that exist independently of our own minds and, indeed, exist independently of any conscious being whatever. Our minds are not immaterial things. We act freely (on many occasions) and such freedom does not require that our minds be "spiritual" or immaterial substances. Nor does such freedom conflict with the fact that we live in a world in which everything that happens is caused to happen by something that happened previously. There is no good reason to believe—though many people do believe—in the existence of supernatural beings, or that any person will survive the destruction of his or her body. With the exception of the portion of the world that consists of our thoughts, the world is what it is—is the way it is—quite independently of what we think. This means that we can make mistakes. No doubt my metaphysical position contains mistakes. I invite the reader to show this.

Suggestions for Further Reading

Chapter 1: Metaphysics

There is a nice account of what philosophy is in *Philosophical Problems and Arguments: An Introduction,* ed. by James W. Cornman, Keith Lehrer, and George S. Pappas (Macmillan, New York, 1982). For more about the branch of philosophy known as ontology, see D. W. Hamlyn, *Metaphysics,* Chapter 3 (Cambridge University Press, Cambridge, England, 1984). See also W. V. O. Quine, *From a Logical Point of View* (Harvard University Press, Cambridge, Mass., 1953). Concerning the nature of metaphysics, see A. J. Ayer, *Metaphysics and Common Sense* (Macmillan, New York, 1969).

Chapter 2: Idealism

There is no better place to begin than with Berkeley's *Principles of Human Knowledge,* ed. by Colin M. Turbayne (Bobbs-Merrill, New York, 1957). G. J. Warnock's *Berkeley* (Penguin Books, Middlesex, England, 1969) is a good secondary source, as is Anthony Flew's *An Introduction to Western Philosophy* (Bobbs-Merrill, New York, 1971), Chapter 10. See also Benson Mates, "Our Knowledge of the External World," in *Skeptical Essays* (University of Chicago Press, Chicago, Illinois, 1981). For a recent defense of idealism, see John Foster's *The Case for Idealism* (Routledge & Kegan Paul, London, 1982).

Chapter 3: Material Minds

Perhaps the best place to begin is with Descartes's "Second Meditation," in *Descartes: Philosophical Writings,* ed. by Elizabeth Anscombe and Peter Geach (Bobbs-Merrill, New York, 1971). For a clear and concise account of different theories of the mind, see David Armstrong's *A Materialist Theory of Mind* (Routledge & Kegan Paul, London, 1968). See also Colin McGinn's *The Character of Mind* (Oxford University Press, Oxford, England, 1982), and *Materialism and the Mind-Body Problem,* ed. by David M. Rosenthal (Prentice-Hall, Englewood Cliffs, New Jersey, 1971).

Chapter 4: Substance

See Aristotle's "Metaphysics," in *The Basic Works of Aristotle,* ed. by Richard McKeon (Random House, New York, 1941). Another good place to begin is with Bertrand Russell, *The Problems of Philosophy,* Chapters 8-11 (Oxford University Press, Oxford, England, 1959). See also G. J. Warnock's *Berkeley,* Chapters 9 and 10 (Pelican Books, London, 1969); D. M. Armstrong's *Nominalism & Realism* (Cambridge University Press, Cambridge, England, 1978); Michael J. Loux's *Substance and Attribute* (D. Reidel, Dordrecht, Holland, 1978); Chapter 5 of Nicholas Jolley's *Leibniz and Locke* (Oxford University Press, Oxford, England, 1986), and Part 1 of Anthony Quinton's *The Nature of Things* (Routledge & Kegan Paul, London, 1973).

Chapter 5: Parts and Wholes

A nice place to begin is with "Leibnizian Substances," in Benson Mates's *The Philosophy of Leibniz* (Oxford University Press, Oxford, England, 1986). David Hume's *A Treatise of Human Nature,* ed. by L. A. Selby-Bigge (Oxford University Press, Oxford, England, 1960), Book 1, Part 4, section 6, provides rich material. See also Descartes's famous discussion of a piece of wax in *Descartes: Philosophical Writings,* ed. by Elizabeth Anscombe and Peter Geach (Bobbs-Merrill, New York, 1971), pp. 72-75. See also Roderick M. Chisholm's *Person and Object* (Open Court, La Salle, Illinois, 1976), Chapter 3 and Appendix B, and Michael A. Slote's *Metaphysics and Essence* (New York University Press, New York, 1975), Chapter 7.

Chapter 6: Change

For a discussion of classical problems concerning motion, see Adolf Grunbaum's *Modern Science and Zeno's Paradoxes* (Wesleyan University Press, Middletown, Connecticut, 1967). For discussions of qualitative and mereological change, see John Locke, *An Essay Concerning Human Understanding,* Book 2, Chapter 27, and Book 3, Chapter 6, ed. by Alexander Campbell Fraser (Dover Publications, New York, 1959). For an interesting account of Locke's position, see J. L. Mackie, *Problems From Locke* (Clarendon Press, Oxford, England, 1976), Chapters 5 and 6. See also David Wiggins, *Sameness and Substance* (Harvard University Press, Cambridge, Massachusetts, 1980), pp. 90-99; Sydney Shoemaker's "Time Without Change," in *Identity, Cause and Mind* (Cambridge University Press, Cambridge, England, 1984); Michael A. Slote, *Metaphysics and Essence,* Chapter 2 (New York University Press, New York, 1975), and G. E. Moore's "External and Internal Relations," in *Philosophical Studies* (Routledge & Kegan Paul, London, 1965).

Chapter 7: Personal Identity

For an excellent anthology containing classical material, see John Perry's *Personal Identity* (University of California Press, Berkeley, 1975). See also

Derek Parfit's *Reasons and Persons* (Oxford University Press, Oxford, England, 1984), Part 3.

Chapter 8: Responsibility

A good beginning is with Harry G. Frankfurt's "Freedom of the Will and the Concept of a Person," in *The Journal of Philosophy,* 67 (January 1971). For more concerning minds and machines see Keith Gunderson's *Mentality and Machines* (Doubleday, New York, 1971). See also Joel Feinberg's *Doing & Deserving* (Princeton University Press, Princeton, New Jersey, 1970) and John Martin Fischer's anthology *Moral Responsibility* (Cornell University Press, Ithaca, New York, 1986).

Chapter 9: Causal Determinism

Many of the relevant issues are clearly presented and discussed in Robert Nozick's *Philosophical Explanations* (Harvard University Press, Cambridge, Massachusetts, 1981), Part 4. Also see J. L. Mackie's *The Cement of the Universe* (Oxford University Press, Oxford, England, 1980); Peter Van Inwagen's *An Essay on Free Will* (Clarendon Press, Oxford, England, 1983) and Alvin I. Goldman's *A Theory of Human Action* (Princeton University Press, Princeton, New Jersey, 1970), Chapters 3 and 6 especially.

Chapter 10: Fate

An excellent place to begin is Stephen Cahn's *Fate, Logic and Time* (Yale University Press, New Haven, Connecticut, 1967). See also Gilbert Ryle's essay "It Was to Be," in *Dilemmas* (Cambridge University Press, Cambridge, England, 1960) and Alvin I. Goldman's *A Theory of Human Action* (Princeton University Press, Princeton, New Jersey, 1970), Chapter 6.

Chapter 11: God

A nice starting point is with David Hume's *Dialogues Concerning Natural Religion* (Hafner Publishing Co., New York, 1961). See also Philip Kitcher's *Abusing Science* (M.I.T. Press, Cambridge, Massachusetts, 1982); Alvin Plantinga's *God and Other Minds* (Cornell University Press, Ithaca, New York, 1967); Anthony Kenny's *The God of the Philosophers* (Oxford University Press, Oxford, England, 1986), and an anthology edited by Thomas V. Morris, *The Concept of God* (Oxford University Press, Oxford, England, 1987). For an interesting defense of Pascal's approach, see William G. Lycan and George N. Schlesinger, "You Bet Your Life: Pascal's Wager Defended," in

Reason and Responsibility, Seventh Edition, ed. by Joel Feinberg (Wadsworth, Belmont, California, 1989).

Chapter 12: Being Realistic

For an interesting attack upon "metaphysical realism," see Chapter 3 of Hilary Putnam's book *Reason, Truth and History* (Cambridge University Press, Cambridge, England, 1981). For quite a different view, see Michael Devitt's *Realism and Truth* (Basil Blackwell, Oxford, England, 1984).

Notes

Chapter 1: Metaphysics

1. Anthony Quinton, *The Nature of Things* (Routledge & Kegan Paul, London, 1973), p. 235.
2. Gilbert Harmon, *Thought* (Princeton University Press, Princeton, N.J., 1973), p. 45.
3. For more about the mind-independence of Fregean concepts, see Raymond Bradley and Norman Swartz, *Possible Worlds: An Introduction to Logic and its Philosophy* (Hackett, Indianapolis, 1979), p. 88. There is, to be sure, a natural tendency to locate concepts in minds. If we regard concepts as meanings of words and hold that meanings of words are ideas in the mind, we are committed to holding that concepts are in the mind. See William Alston, *The Philosophy of Language* (Prentice-Hall, Englewood Cliffs, N.J., 1964), chapter 1.
4. See P. L. Heath, "Concept," in *The Encyclopedia of Philosophy,* ed. by Paul Edwards (Macmillan: New York, 1967), and Bradley and Swartz, pp. 87–91.
5. Robert Kraut, "Sensory States and Sensory Objects," *Nous* 16 (1982), pp. 277–293.
6. This is only the barest sketch of one of many approaches to the matter. See W. V. Quine and J. S. Ullian, *The Web of Belief* (Random House, New York, 1978), and William G. Lycan, *Judgment and Justification* (M.I.T. Press, Cambridge, Mass., 1988).
7. Some theorists argue that it is rational to believe in God whether or not there is anything like a "proof" of God's existence. See Blaise Pascal, "The Wager," in *Thoughts,* translated by W. F. Trotter (Dutton, New York, 1910).
8. If the concept of God is inconsistent, then nothing could satisfy this concept. See David Blumenfeld, "On the Compossibility of the Divine Attributes," in *The Concept of God,* ed. by Thomas V. Morris (Oxford University Press, Oxford, England, 1987).
9. Paul M. Churchland, *Scientific Realism and the Plasticity of the Mind* (Cambridge University Press, Cambridge, England, 1979), p. 23.
10. Richard Taylor, *Metaphysics* (Prentice-Hall, Englewood Cliffs, N.J., 1963), p. 2.

Chapter 2: Idealism

1. G. E. Moore, *Philosophical Studies* (Routledge & Kegan Paul, London, 1922), p. 16.

2. George Berkeley, *A Treatise Concerning the Principles of Human Knowledge,* originally published in 1710 (Bobbs-Merrill, New York, 1957), p. 39.
3. *The Philosophical Works of Descartes,* translated by Elizabeth S. Haldane and G. R. T. Ross, vol. I (Cambridge University Press, Cambridge, England, 1968), pp. 145–146.
4. G. J. Warnock, *Berkeley* (Penguin Books, Middlesex, England, 1969), pp. 145–146.
5. Berkeley's *Treatise,* pp. 36–37.
6. Warnock, *Berkeley,* pp. 89–90.
7. Gottlob Frege, "The Thought: A Logical Inquiry," in *Philosophical Logic,* ed. by P. F. Strawson (Oxford University Press, Oxford, England, 1967), pp. 27–28.
8. John Foster, "Berkeley on the Physical World," in *Essays on Berkeley,* ed. by Foster and Howard Robinson (Oxford University Press, Oxford, England, 1985), p. 94.
9. See Foster, p. 95, and Warnock, pp. 123–124.
10. Saul A. Kripke, *Naming and Necessity* (Harvard University Press, Cambridge, Mass., 1980), p. 128.
11. Foster, p. 85.

Chapter 3: Material Minds

1. David Armstrong, *A Materialist Theory of Mind* (Routledge & Kegan Paul, London, 1968), p. 73.
2. Armstrong, p. 6.
3. See Sydney Shoemaker's interesting discussion of the view that a person is a "partly physical system" in *Identity, Cause and Mind* (Cambridge University Press, Cambridge, Mass., 1984), pp. 139–158.
4. Not the queen we read about in history books but a mere princess, a student of Descartes's and, according to some, the great love of his life. See Elizabeth Anscombe and Peter Thomas Geach, *Descartes: Philosophical Writings* (Bobbs-Merrill, New York, 1971), p. xxxv.
5. Anscombe and Geach, pp. 274–275.
6. Peter Smith and O. R. Jones, *The Philosophy of Mind* (Cambridge University Press, Cambridge, England, 1986), pp. 52–57.
7. Armstrong, pp. 157–158.
8. Thomas Nagel, *Mortal Questions* (Cambridge University Press, Cambridge, England, 1979), pp. 169–170.
9. See two papers by David Lewis, "An Argument for the Identity Theory" and "Mad Pain and Martian Pain" in *Philosophical Papers,* vol. I (Oxford University Press, Oxford, England, 1983).
10. Wittgenstein argued against the possibility of private languages containing terms whose meaning is accessible only to a single speaker. See *Philosophical Investigations* (Macmillan, New York, 1953). See also the

papers on privacy by A. J. Ayer, R. Rhees, and John Cook in *Wittgenstein: A Collection of Critical Essays,* ed. by George Pitcher (Doubleday, Garden City, N.Y., 1966).

11. Donald Davidson, "Psychology as Philosophy," in *The Philosophy of Mind,* ed. by Jonathan Glover (Oxford University Press, Oxford, England, 1976), p. 102.

12. Wallace I. Matson, *Sentience* (University of California Press, Berkeley, Calif., 1976), pp. 171–172.

Chapter 4: Substance

1. David Armstrong, *Nominalism & Realism* (Cambridge University Press, Cambridge, England, 1978), vol. I, p. 115.

2. Michael Devitt, *Realism & Truth* (Blackwell, Oxford, England, 1984), p. 13.

3. G. E. Moore, *Some Main Problems of Philosophy* (Collier Books, New York, 1962), pp. 37, 317.

4. Berkeley thinks his position is perfectly consistent with common sense. "I do not argue against the existence of any one thing that we can apprehend either by sense or reflection." *Principles of Human Knowledge* (Bobbs-Merrill, New York, 1957), p. 39.

5. Sound waves from a falling tree are present whether or not anyone is present to "hear" them. Some theorists suggest that things are fundamentally different when we turn to microscopic entities such as photons. See Fred Alan Wolf, *Taking the Quantum Leap* (Harper & Row, San Francisco, 1981), pp. 200–201.

6. Not every class determines or represents a distinct kind of thing. Question: what is distinctive of classes that do represent kinds? One answer is defended by Baruch A. Brody in *Identity and Essence* (Princeton University Press, Princeton, N.J., 1980). Roughly, Brody would say that some classes are such that their members cannot fail to be members of the class in question. All and only such classes represent kinds.

7. Moore in *Some Main Problems,* p. 28.

8. *Some Main Problems,* p. 29.

9. *Some Main Problems,* p. 29.

10. "Aristotle's *Categories,"* translated by J. L. Ackrill, in *Aristotle,* ed. by J. M. E. Moravcsik (Doubleday, Garden City, N.Y., 1967), pp. 92–93.

11. See Armstrong's interesting discussion of "concept nominalism," in chapter 2 of *Nominalism & Realism,* vol. I (Cambridge University Press, Cambridge, England, 1978).

12. D. M. MacKinnon, "Aristotle's Conception of Substance," in *New Essays on Plato and Aristotle,* ed. by Renford Bambrough (Humanities Press, New York, 1965), p. 100.

13. John Locke, *An Essay Concerning Human Understanding,* vol. II, ed. by

Alexander Campbell Fraser (Dover Press, New York, 1959). The work was first published in 1690.

14. Locke's *Essay*, vol. II.

15. There is a good deal of controversy concerning precisely what view of substance Locke held. See M. R. Ayers, "The Ideas of Power and Substance in Locke's Philosophy," *The Philosophical Quarterly*, vol. 25 (January 1975), and Jonathan Bennett, "Substratum," in *History of Philosophy Quarterly*, vol. 4 (April 1987).

16. Locke's *Essay*, vol. II, p. 397.

17. Bertrand Russell, *An Inquiry into Meaning and Truth* (Allen & Unwin, London, 1940), pp. 97–98.

18. See David Armstrong, *Nominalism & Realism*, vol. I, chapters 8 and 9, and Douglas C. Long, "Particulars and Their Qualities," *The Philosophy Quarterly*, vol. 18 (July 1968).

19. See Max Black's "The Identity of Indiscernibles," in *Problems of Analysis* (Routledge & Kegan Paul, London, 1954).

20. Plato argued that "forms" have reality apart from individual things that "participate" in forms. If properties of things are taken to be Platonic forms, then Plato's view is that properties have reality apart from the various things that instantiate or participate in properties.

Chapter 5: Parts and Wholes

1. John F. Post, *The Faces of Existence* (Cornell University Press, Ithaca, N.Y., 1987), p. 286.

2. Robert Nozick, *Philosophical Explanations* (Harvard University Press, Cambridge, Mass., 1981), p. 100.

3. George Berkeley, *A Treatise Concerning the Principles of Human Knowledge*, originally published in 1710 (Bobbs-Merrill, N.Y., 1957), p. 86.

4. Sir Arthur Eddington, "Two Tables," in *Philosophy: The Basic Issues*, ed. by E. D. Klemke, A. David Kline, and Robert Hollinger (St. Martin's Press, New York, 1982).

5. Jeremy Bernstein, "Personal History," *The New Yorker*, February 2, 1987, p. 62.

6. *The Philosophical Works of Descartes*, ed. by Elizabeth S. Haldane and G. R. T. Ross, vol. I (Cambridge University Press, Cambridge, England, 1968), p. 239.

7. See Robert Merrihew Adams, "Phenomenalism and Corporeal Substance in Leibniz," in *Midwest Studies in Philosophy*, vol. VIII (1983), ed. by Peter A. French, Theodore E. Uehling, Jr., and Howard K. Wettstein (University of Minnesota Press, Minneapolis, Minn., 1983), p. 222.

8. See Noel Fleming, "On Leibniz on Subject and Substance," *The Philosophical Review* XCVI (January 1987), p. 85.

9. Leibniz in correspondence with Arnauld, in *Leibniz: Basic Writings*, translated by George R. Montgomery (Open Court, La Salle, Ill., 1962), p. 220.

10. Adams, "Phenomenalism and Corporeal Substance in Leibniz."

11. Fleming, p. 85.

12. *Leibniz: Basic Writings,* p. 58.

13. Compare Keith Campbell, *Metaphysics: An Introduction* (Dickenson, Encino, Calif., 1976), p. 31.

14. David H. Sanford, "Infinite Regress Arguments," in *Principles of Philosophical Reasoning,* ed. by James H. Fetzer (Rowman & Allanheld, Totowa, N.J., 1984), p. 109.

15. David Armstrong, *Nominalism & Realism,* vol. I (Cambridge University Press, Cambridge, England, 1980), p. 82.

16. Armstrong argues that genuine parts of a substance are substances.

17. Edwin Hartman, "Essentialism and Semantic Theory in Aristotle," *The Philosophical Review* LXXXV (October 1976), p. 548.

18. "Aristotle's Categories," translated by J. L. Ackrill, in *Aristotle,* ed. by J. M. E. Moravcsik (Doubleday, Garden City, N.Y., 1967), p. 98.

19. *Leibniz: Basic Writings,* p. 223.

Chapter 6: Change

1. Sydney Shoemaker, *Identity, Cause and Mind* (Cambridge University Press, Cambridge, England, 1984), p. 142.

2. D. H. Mellor, *Real Time* (Cambridge University Press, Cambridge, England, 1981), p. 110.

3. Moore, *Some Main Problems of Philosophy* (Collier Books, New York, 1953), p. 147.

4. Locke argues that when even one particle is added to or removed from a mass of matter, we are left with a new, numerically different mass of matter. Locke might say the same thing about piles of dirty laundry.

5. See John Perry, "Relative Identity and Number," *Canadian Journal of Philosophy,* vol. VIII (March 1978), p. 7.

6. See Richard Sharvey, "Things," in *The Monist* 53 (July 1969).

Chapter 7: Personal Identity

1. Thomas Nagel, *The View from Nowhere* (Oxford University Press, Oxford, England, 1986), p. 40.

2. David Wiggins, *Sameness and Substance* (Harvard University Press, Cambridge, Mass., 1980).

3. Peter Smith and O. R. Jones, *The Philosophy of Mind* (Cambridge University Press, Cambridge, England, 1986), p. 77.

4. Smith and Jones, p. 76.
5. Baruch A. Brody, *Identity and Essence* (Princeton University Press, Princeton, N.J., 1980).
6. Michael Tooley, *Abortion and Infanticide* (Oxford University Press, Oxford, England, 1983), p. 347.
7. Tooley, p. 395.
8. *Descartes: Philosophical Writings*, ed. by Anscombe and Geach, p. 69.
9. Derek Parfit, *Reasons and Persons* (Oxford University Press, Oxford, England, 1984), p. 199.
10. John Locke, "Of Identity and Diversity," in *Personal Identity*, ed. by John Perry (University of California Press, Berkeley, Calif., 1975), p. 40.
11. "Of Memory," in Perry's *Personal Identity*, p. 114.
12. Derek Parfit, "Personal Identity" in Perry, p. 203.
13. Parfit, *Reasons and Persons*, p. 206.
14. Sydney Shoemaker, *Identity, Cause and Mind* (Cambridge University Press, Cambridge, England, 1984), pp. 139–158.
15. Smith and Jones, *The Philosophy of Mind*, p. 71.
16. Smith and Jones, *The Philosophy of Mind*, pp. 80–81.
17. For more concerning this sort of case, see Parfit in *Reasons and Persons*, pp. 254–256.
18. Thomas Nagel, *Mortal Questions* (Cambridge University Press, Cambridge, England, 1979), p. 7.

Chapter 8: Responsibility

1. Richard Swinburne and Sydney Shoemaker, *Personal Identity* (Blackwell, Oxford, England, 1984), p. 31.
2. Michael E. Levin, *Metaphysics and the Mind-Body Problem* (Oxford University Press, Oxford, England, 1979), p. 227.
3. Alvin I. Goldman, *A Theory of Human Action* (Princeton University Press, Princeton, N.J., 1970), pp. 172–173.
4. *The Philosophical Works of Descartes*, translated by Elizabeth S. Haldane and G. R. T. Ross, vol. I, p. 116. See also Anthony Kenny, *Descartes* (Random House, New York, 1968), p. 201.
5. Wallace I. Matson, *Sentience* (University of California Press, Berkeley, 1976), p. 166.
6. Levin, *Metaphysics and the Mind-Body Problem*, p. 217.
7. William G. Lycan, *Consciousness* (M.I.T. Press, Cambridge, Mass., 1987), p. 125.
8. Gilbert Ryle argues that the mind is not a substance in *The Concept of Mind* (Barnes & Noble, New York, 1949).

9. David Hume, *A Treatise of Human Nature,* ed. by L. A. Selby-Bigge (Oxford University Press, Oxford, England, 1960), p. 207.

10. Nelson Pike, "Hume's Bundle Theory of the Self: A Limited Defense," in *The American Philosophical Quarterly,* vol. 4 (April 1967).

11. Hume, *Treatise of Human Nature,* p. 207.

12. Derek Parfit, *Reasons and Persons* (Oxford University Press, Oxford, England, 1984), p. 275.

13. For more about category mistakes, see Ryle in *The Concept of Mind.*

14. But critics ask: What is it that does the observing?

15. Roderick M. Chisholm, "On the Observability of the Self," *Philosophy and Phenomenological Research,* vol. XXX (September 1969), p. 9.

16. Cf. Pike in "Hume's Bundle Theory of the Self."

17. D. H. Mellor, *Real Time* (Cambridge University Press, Cambridge, England, 1981), p. 106.

Chapter 9: Causal Determinism

1. Peter Van Inwagen, *An Essay on Free Will* (Oxford University Press, Oxford, England, 1984), p. 2.

2. Daniel C. Dennett, *Elbow Room* (M.I.T. Press, Cambridge, Mass., 1984), p. 154.

3. David Lewis, "Counterfactual Dependence and Time's Arrow," *Nous* 13 (1979), p. 459.

4. *The Philosophical Works of Descartes,* vol. I, ed. by Elizabeth S. Haldane and G. R. T. Ross (Cambridge University Press, Cambridge, England, 1968), p. 116.

5. John Locke, *An Essay Concerning Human Understanding,* ed. by Alexander Campbell Fraser, vol. I (Dover, New York, 1959), p. 329.

6. John Searle, *Minds, Brains and Science* (Harvard University Press, Cambridge, Mass., 1984).

7. Michael Slote, "Selective Necessity and the Free-Will Problem," in *The Journal of Philosophy,* 1982.

8. Locke, *Essay,* p. 329.

9. Locke, *Essay,* pp. 319–328.

10. Locke, *Essay,* p. 328.

11. Note Frazer's comments concerning Jonathan Edwards in Locke's *Essay,* vol. I, p. 328n.

12. Van Inwagen argues that universal causation does not entail determinism in *An Essay on Free Will.*

13. David Hume, *A Treatise of Human Nature,* ed. by Silby-Bigge (Oxford University Press, Oxford, England, 1960), pp. 170–172.

14. Hume, *Treatise,* pp. 163–168.

Chapter 10: Fate

1. Benson Mates, *The Philosophy of Leibniz* (Oxford University Press, Oxford, England, 1986), p. 113.
2. See Masiji Ibuse's *Black Rain* (Bantam Books, New York, 1985).
3. "Is God a Taoist?" Raymond M. Smullyan, in *The Mind's I,* ed. by Douglas R. Hofstader and Daniel C. Dennett (Basic Books, New York, 1981), p. 333.
4. Noel Fleming, "On Leibniz on Subject and Substance," *The Philosophical Review,* XCVI (January 1987), p. 97.
5. Mates, p. 84.
6. Cited by E. M. Curley, "The Root of Contingency," in *Leibniz: A Collection of Critical Essays,* ed. by Harry G. Frankfurt (Doubleday, New York, 1972), p. 83. See also Mates, *The Philosophy of Leibniz.*
7. See Ian Hacking, "A Leibnizian Theory of Truth," in *Leibniz: Critical and Interpretative Essays,* ed. by Michael Hooker (University of Minnesota Press, Minneapolis, Minn., 1982).
8. Mates, p. 84.

Chapter 11: God

1. Anthony Kenny, *The God of the Philosophers* (Oxford University Press, Oxford, England, 1986), p. 5.
2. David Hume, "Dialogues Concerning Natural Religion," in *Reason and Responsibility,* ed. by Joel Feinberg (Wadsworth, Belmont, Calif., 1985), p. 39.
3. Hume's "Dialogues."
4. Hume's "Dialogues."
5. See Richard Dawkins, *The Blind Watchmaker* (Norton, New York, 1987).
6. *Descartes: Philosophical Writings,* ed. by Elizabeth Anscombe and Peter Geach (Bobbs-Merrill, New York, 1954), p. 103.
7. Norman Malcolm, "Anselm's Ontological Arguments," in *Knowledge and Certainty* (Prentice-Hall, Englewood Cliffs, N.J., 1963), p. 145.
8. Thomas V. Morris, "Properties, Modalities, and God," in *The Philosophical Review,* XCIII (January 1984), pp. 44–45.

Chapter 12: Being Realistic

1. Elliot Sober, "Realism and Independence," *Nous,* XVI (September 1982), p. 369.
2. Hartrey Field, "Realism and Relativism," *The Journal of Philosophy* LLXXIX (October 1982), p. 553.

3. Moore, *Some Main Problems of Philosophy* (Collier Books, New York, 1953), p. 30.

4. As noted in Chapter 1, some theorists hold that common sense may, and indeed often does, play us false. See Paul M. Churchland, *Scientific Realism and the Plasticity of the Mind* (Cambridge University Press, Cambridge, England, 1979).

5. J. J. C. Smart, *Between Science and Philosophy* (Random House, New York, 1968), pp. 230–233.

6. Michael Dummett, "Common Sense and Physics," in *Perception and Identity*, ed. by G. F. Macdonald (Cornell University Press, Ithaca, N.Y., 1979), p. 18.

7. Ludwig Wittgenstein, *Tractatus Logico-Philosophicus,* translated by D. F. Pears and B. F. McGuinness (Routledge & Kegan Paul, London, England, 1961), p. 7.

8. H. Putnam, *Philosophical Papers: Reason, Truth, and History,* vol. 3 (Cambridge University Press, Cambridge, England), p. 130.

9. Field, "Reason and Relativism," p. 556.

10. William P. Alston, "Yes, Virginia, There Is a Real World," Presidential Address to the Western Division of the American Philosophical Association, in *Proceedings and Addresses of The American Philosophical Association,* vol. 52 (August 1979), p. 787.

11. Dummett, "Common Sense and Physics," p. 4.

12. Putnam, *Reason, Truth, and History,* p. 6.

13. For more about the vat hypothesis, see Anthony L. Brueckner, "Brains in a Vat," *The Journal of Philosophy,* LXXXIII (March 1986).

14. Putnam, *Reason, Truth, and History,* p. 49.

15. Moore, *Some Main Problems of Philosophy,* p. 321.

16. Putnam, *Meaning and the Moral Sciences* (Routledge & Kegan Paul, Boston, 1978), p. 125.

17. Putnam, *Reason, Truth, and History,* p. 200.

18. Putnam, *Reason, Truth, and History,* p. 73.

19. David Hume, *A Treatise of Human Nature* (Oxford University Press, Oxford, England, 1960), p. 271.

*I*ndex

About the Author

William R. Carter is Professor of Philosophy at North Carolina State University in Raleigh. A recipient of a National Endowment for the Humanities Fellowship, Professor Carter currently is working on a book addressing metaphysical problems of survival and identity. He received his Ph.D. at the University of Virginia. Papers by the author on metaphysical issues have appeared in *The Philosophical Review*, *Midwest Studies in Philosophy*, *Mind*, and *Philosophical Studies*.